DID NOT FINISH

Misadventures in Running, Cycling and Swimming
(Book One in the DNF Series)

George Mahood

This edition published 2021 by George Mahood.

www.facebook.com/georgemahood
www.instagram.com/georgemahood
www.twitter.com/georgemahood
www.georgemahood.com

ONE

My phone buzzed on the kitchen counter. It was my wife, Rachel.

'Hello,' I answered cheerily.

She didn't respond. I only heard rustling.

'Hellooo,' I said again, and could make out the plodding of her feet along the road.

Rachel had gone out for a run and must have somehow butt-dialled me mid-jog. She often butt-dialled me, but usually from somewhere boring like the supermarket. She occasionally called me mid-run to inform me she was lost, and could I tell her where she was? Or she had sustained an injury, and could she have a lift? Or to ask if she had left her hair-straighteners on? Or she was in a field full of inquisitive cows, and what was I going to do about it? But those calls were all deliberate. This was the first accidental live-action running butt-dial I had ever received.

'Hellooooooo.'

'What are you doing, Daddy?' asked Kitty – aged four and the youngest of our three children – as she joined me in the kitchen.

'I'm listening to Mummy running. She's phoned me by

mistake. Here, listen,' I said, as I put my phone on speakerphone.

'HELLOOO! RACHEL... HELLOOOOO!' I said, a little louder this time. Her pace seemed to quicken and became more erratic. Perhaps she had reached the top of a hill. Or the start of a Strava segment.

'RAAACHEEELLL!' I shouted, and her footfall became even louder and more frantic. Her breathing was now extremely audible, and she started wheezing and gasping for breath. My smile faded. *What if she hadn't phoned me by accident? What if she was in trouble?*

'Rachel? Are you alright?'

The running sounds stopped suddenly, but the wheezing continued.

Oh my god. This could be serious. Should I go out looking for her? Or call the police?

'RACHEL? WHAT'S GOING ON? ARE YOU OK?' I said, with panic now in my voice.

We then heard the sounds of more fumbling, and the phone went dead.

'Is Mummy ok?' asked Kitty. 'What happened?'

Our other two children – Leo (aged 6) and Layla (aged 8) – appeared from the other room after hearing me shouting.

'What's going on?' said Layla.

'Mummy just phoned me while she was running.'

I was just about to call her back when my phone vibrated again.

'Rachel? Are you ok?'

'Erm... yes...' she panted. 'I think so.'

'What happened? We were worried about you.'

'Did you just ring me?'

'No, you just rang me.'

'Not now, I mean a minute ago. Did you ring me?'

'No, you rang me. You must have butt-dialled me.'

'Were you talking to me?'

'Yes! For several minutes!'

'Oh, thank god for that,' she said, and then began laughing manically.

'Why? What happened?'

'I was running along, and I started hearing this strange voice saying *HELLO* to me, and I thought someone was hiding in the hedge. I'm in the middle of nowhere and it really freaked me out.'

'Ha, is that why you were running so fast?'

'YES! Could you hear that?'

'Yes, it sounded like you were full on sprinting.'

'I really was! I thought there was some freaky weirdo in the bushes, and I was trying to get away from whoever it was as quickly as possible. But it didn't matter how fast I ran; the voice was still there. And then he started calling me by my name, which was terrifying.'

'That's so funny. Did you not find it weird that the voice kept going, even when you kept running?'

'Yes! But I assumed it was some madman racing along on the other side of the hedge alongside me.'

'Ha, you are such a weirdo.'

'You're the one with the creepy phone voice who sounds like a madman.'

'That's my normal voice. You've never complained about it before.'

'You've never been spying on me from a hedge before!'

'I wasn't in a hedge!'

'Anyway, I think I probably got a personal best up that last hill.'

I have been a reluctant runner since training for my first marathon in 2009. Although rarely enjoying the actual process of running, I loved the feeling and the satisfaction of finishing a run and seeing my fitness gradually improve.

I often suggested to Rachel that she try running, knowing she too would feel the same benefits. But she had a list of excuses on hand each time to dismiss the idea:

I don't have time.

I am not a runner.

I'm too unfit.

I'm too tired.

I can't be bothered.

One day, before we had kids, she decided to give it a try. Just to shut me up. Rather than begin with a gentle jog around the block, she completed a distance of about two miles, which was the furthest she had ever run.

'How was it? How do you feel?' I asked when she came panting through the door.

'AWFUL! I HATED IT!'

'Are you glad you went?'

'NO! Not at all. It was a massive waste of time! I feel horrendous and I don't feel any fitter.'

'You've been for one run. You're not going to feel fitter after one run.'

'Well, I thought it would at least make me feel good.'

'Give it a chance.'

She made a chuffing sound as though I was fabricating the enormous body of scientific evidence linking exercise with improved physical and mental health.

But not wanting to give up that easily, she went out and did the same run the following day, and again burst in through the front door gasping for breath.

'Good run?'

'NO! It was WORSE than yesterday. WHEN am I going to start feeling fitter?'

'Err... I think it will take more than two runs. And maybe if you build up slowly and perhaps go for shorter runs. And maybe not consecutive days to begin with.'

She nodded at my suggestion and then ignored it completely. Frustrated that she still didn't feel fitter after two runs, and too impatient to wait, she went out running again later that same day. Then she went twice the following day and twice the day after that.

She returned from each run having hated it even more than the day before. I warned her she was overdoing it, but she said she didn't have time to ease into it gradually. She was determined to defy science and achieve peak physical fitness within a week. After six days and a total of about ten runs (which was more runs than she had done in the previous 28 years of her life combined), she had developed agonising pain in her legs – most likely shin splints – and could barely walk, let alone run.

'SEE! I TOLD YOU RUNNING WAS NOT FOR ME!' she shouted. 'YOU SAID I WOULD FEEL GREAT! WHY DID YOU MAKE ME TAKE UP RUNNING? NOW I CAN'T EVEN WALK!'

'Firstly, I didn't make you go running. And I think maybe you overdid it just a little. Give your legs a chance to get better and then maybe you could try running once or twice a week instead.'

'No, I'm not doing it again. Running is not for me. I'm DONE with running.'

True to her word, for the next five years, Rachel didn't once quicken her step beyond a walk.

In 2013 we moved to Devon, and something changed. I don't know whether it was the new environment, a renewed desire to get fit, the children all being a little bit older and slightly less high maintenance, or perhaps just a need to have some time alone and away from them (and me), but Rachel gave running another go. I cannot claim she finally gave in to my peer pressure, because I had given up suggesting it a long time ago.

After Rachel's first run in Devon, she came in through

the front door puffing and panting as she had before, but this time there was a subtle glimmer of positivity about her. I obviously didn't dare say this to her at the time, choosing to keep quiet instead, but it was almost like she had enjoyed herself.

Rachel's running romance was short-lived, however. Her all-or-nothing mentality took over once again, and she began running every day. Again, her body protested, and she was soon injured like before and unable to walk without pain. But this time it was different. This time she didn't declare that she would never run again. This time she admitted she had overdone it. This time she was keen to rest her injury and get back to running again.

After a few weeks, Rachel's legs recovered enough to try again, and this time she finally took my advice and built up slowly. A few months later, she ran her first 10k in Plymouth and loved it – even though I somehow lost her stopwatch minutes before the start. She then ran her first half-marathon in Torbay and enjoyed that too. So, I signed her up for her first marathon in Edinburgh – without her knowing and despite her insistence that she would NEVER run a marathon – and she loved it. From then on, she was hooked.

Our roles had reversed, and Rachel was now firmly established as the runner in our family. She was the one to now regularly encourage me to head out the front door for a run. But not with her, though. She loved running but didn't like running with me. She said I was too quick for her (I wasn't) and she found me too talkative and annoying (I probably was) and she preferred the silence and solitude of running solo.

And if I'm honest, so did I.

TWO

Very, very occasionally, if the children were at school, and we were both heading out for a run at the same time, Rachel would suggest we go together. I learned not to talk too much as I knew it annoyed her, and I made sure I let her set the pace so she couldn't accuse me of being too fast. We took part in a couple of 10ks, but I thought there was little chance Rachel and I would ever get to the stage where we could run a marathon together. During her Edinburgh marathon, she got the rage with me when I offered words of encouragement from the side-lines, so I imagined she would completely lose her shit over the course of 26.2 miles running side by side.

But perhaps it could be good for our relationship? It would certainly be a challenge, and it could either make or break us.

While mindlessly scrolling through social media one evening, I saw a link to a marathon I had never heard of before: the Salcombe Coastal Marathon. This was a small, low-key event that took place along the challenging South West Coast Path either side of the town of Salcombe in Devon. It was entirely off-road and an extremely tough course, which meant our expectations of our finishing time would be considerably lower. I casually suggested to Rachel that we run it together. To my surprise, she agreed.

The race started in the coastal village of Torcross and followed the coast path to the finish in Bantham. To cope with the logistics of runners getting home after the event, we were encouraged to park at the finish and take a provided bus to the start. We arrived at the bus pickup point just in time for the pre-race briefing.

Most of the other entrants seemed to know each other and were members of local Hasher groups. Hashers – or Hash House Harriers, to give them their full title – are a running club who refer to themselves as 'a drinking club with a running problem'. The Hash House Harriers began in 1938 when a group of British officers, stationed in Kuala Lumpur, set up a weekly running club to help them cope with hangovers and gain a thirst for more beer. There are now more than 2,000 Hashing clubs worldwide. Most meet weekly, whatever the weather, at a local pub, and complete a run (predominately cross country) marked out by one of their members, and they all then return to the pub for beer and chips.

The unique aspect of hashing is that a series of markers and arrows are drawn on the ground with flour, guiding the runners around the countryside. Many of these markers are false leads and end at a dead end. The faster runners follow these incorrect directions and then return to the correct route and scrub out the false markers, to allow the slower runners an easier route. All runners should end up returning to the pub at roughly the same time. To choose to spend your cold winter evenings running through fields and streams, following arrows made from flour, often with only a head-torch to light the way, requires an eccentric attitude. This was our first experience of being amongst Hashers and it was quite an awakening.

We soon learned that Hashers do not refer to each other by their actual names. They all have nicknames – given to you by the rest of the club once you've established yourself as a regular member. These nicknames can take any form but are often sexual in nature. It is quite normal to have a well-respected, retired dentist named Clive, who on Wednesday evenings when out hashing, becomes Captain Spunkalot. Or, the treasurer of the local village committee, a 76-year-old florist called Susan, dons her running kit and transforms into Baroness Fanny Flaps. It makes you wonder if the entire Hashers movement is actually just an elaborate cover-up for some senior citizen sex ring.

Before boarding the bus, we gathered for the race briefing and there was lots of banter (or perhaps it was sexual tension) between the other runners. The race organiser, who was named something like Horny Rampant Badger, gave us a quick summary of the route, some safety announcements, and then reeled off a few stats about the event. He told us the course record stood at about 3.5 hours, which was impressive considering the rough terrain, 5000ft of ascent, and the fact that runners have to cross an estuary on a ferry midway through. The record number of pints of beer consumed along the way was 4.5. There were a few nods of approval and positive grunts showing some bravado that this was a record that was set to be beaten today. Horny Rampant Badger also told us that two of the Hashers held some record (I'm not sure what) of having sex halfway through the race. Presumably with each other, although this wasn't clarified. I nudged Rachel and gave her a wink. From the look she gave me, I knew there was more chance of me breaking the 3.5-hour course record.

Horny Rampant Badger also told us that once we got to the start at Torcross, we should make sure the marshal ticked our names off the list and then we were free to start whenever we liked. We would time our own races, which avoided the need for a mass start on the narrow coast path. After hearing it was self-timed, combined with the beer consumption stat, it did make me question the validity of the course record.

It was a beautiful, bright sunny morning by the time we climbed off the bus in Torcross. We chatted briefly in the queue to a couple in their seventies named Jizzy Rascal and Deep Throat Snow Queen, gave our own very boring normal names to the marshal to tick off the list, and set off towards the coast path.

The event had a fun and relaxed feel to it, and within minutes of leaving the village of Torcross, we were down to a slow walk up the steep steps over the headland. Due to the narrowness of many parts of the route, the race was limited to 100 entrants. We followed two runners – Cousin Ball Bag and Auntie Nipple Rat – down into the cove on the other side, before realising we had accidentally strayed from the coast path and trudged back up the steep steps to re-join the route.

We reached the village of Beesands, which was the start and finish of my one and only ultramarathon (featured in my book *Chasing Trails*). From here, we followed the same route as the ultra for the next 11 miles. But conditions could not have been more different. During the ultramarathon, my friend Mark and I experienced 60mph winds, horizontal rain, hail, and knee-deep mud. Today, there was a bright blue sky and just the slightest breath of wind. During the ultra, it was this extreme weather that had added an illogical level of enjoyment to the event, as it helped distract from the pain and suffering of the running. It would be interesting to see how we fared in perfect conditions.

From Beesands, we followed the coast path up and over the headland into the once thriving fishing village of Hallsands which now sits mostly at the bottom of the sea, and then out along the peninsula towards the prominent lighthouse at Start Point. The official coast path cuts inland a little before the lighthouse at Start Point, along a fairly manageable section of path. This was the route we had sensibly followed during the ultramarathon. But not today. In order to make the route a full marathon, no corners could be cut, so we were required to take the alternative option a little further on; a steep rocky ridge with a metal chain for us to hold on to. We hauled ourselves up and over the rocks, dropping down over the other side of the ridge where we eventually met the main path again. Several other runners had opted for the earlier shortcut.

'Why didn't we just take that route instead?' said Rachel. 'That looks much easier.'

'It is, but they are technically cheating.'

'Cheating? They are still following the coast path.'

'Well, it probably won't be a full marathon for them. They are only cheating themselves.'

Rachel rolled her eyes.

The view down the coastline towards Prawle Point as we crested the headland was spectacular. The last time I ran along here there had been no view at all, and it genuinely felt like they were two entirely different places.

'What do you think so far?' I asked Rachel. 'Having fun?'

'It is a little different to Edinburgh, that's for sure.'

'Much more fun, isn't it?'

'I'll let you know later.'

It was an incredible day to be out on the South West Coast Path, and the first half of the race was an absolute joy. We were running at a very slow pace, partly because neither of us were fit enough or experienced enough to traverse the coast path with any speed. But also, because we didn't care how long it took us and we just wanted to enjoy the day as much as possible. There were several steep and rocky up and downs where all runners were reduced to a slow single-file trudge, and it was a relief to be forced to walk these sections.

Rachel seemed to embrace the challenge. She was quiet, which is not usually a good sign. But on this occasion, it seemed to be due to her concentrating on her footing – having rarely done any trail running before – rather than the result of some bubbling inner turmoil. I was keeping my chat to a minimum, just in case.

We passed the pretty beach of Lannacombe, and then along the edge of fields that sit on a raised beach, formed after the last ice age, with the cliffs now set back from the sea to our right.

The aid station below Prawle Point was like nothing I had ever seen at a running event. It was as though they had stolen the buffet from a child's birthday party and moved it to a gazebo on the edge of a cliff. There were bowls of crisps, cakes, sandwiches, biscuits and even Party Rings. I half expected them to wheel out a game of Pin the Tail on the Donkey or begin a round of Pass the Parcel.

'This is amazing. Thank you,' I said to the smiling silver-haired woman manning the station.

'You're welcome. Well done, both of you. Lovely day to be out running,' she said in a soothing voice.

'It is. Although having seen all this food it might be a long time before we get going again,' said Rachel.

I then had a sudden panic.

'This is the feed station for the Salcombe Marathon?' I asked.

'Yes, it is,' she laughed.

'Phew. I was worried we had gate-crashed some kids' party. I probably should have checked before filling a plate.'

'Yes, we got a bit carried away with the food.'

'Are you a Hasher?' I asked.

'I am indeed.'

'Dare I ask what your nickname is?'

'Janet Bum-Bandit,' she said, and I nearly choked on my pretzels.

We thanked Janet Bum-Bandit, took another handful of party food, and snacked on it while we walked up the next hill towards the coastguard station at Prawle Point. To our right, on the hill above us, sat the extraordinary sight of the Coastguard cottages – a row of ten houses, now mostly holiday lets, built in the early 1900s to house coastguard workers. It is a full row of terraced houses, each with its own fenced garden, and it looks like the street could have been transported from any town centre in Britain. High on the cliffs above the ocean, with no other buildings nearby, they look totally out of place, but at the same time utterly perfect.

The coastguard station at East Prawle is manned 365 days a year by a team of over 60 volunteers. Visitors are allowed to pop in and say hello, but we thought it unlikely they would want two sweaty runners in their hut, so continued onward.

The stretch of coastline west of Prawle Point is one of the most beautiful parts of the South West Coast Path I have seen. It is rugged and raw, and you rarely see any other people. The busy town of Salcombe is only a few miles away but hidden by several headlands and separated by a river estuary. On a sunny day, the sea turns turquoise and inviting and it can feel as though you are in some tropical paradise. But when the weather is bad – as it had been the last time I ran this stretch of coast – the water turns black, the waves crash wildly against the rocks and it feels like you're about to witness the apocalypse.

Today it was a tropical paradise. It was late morning, and the sun was blazing down. Despite being early spring, there was still a temptation to run down to one of the many coves we passed and plunge into the sea.

After about two and a half hours, we reached the village of East Portlemouth, which sits near the mouth of the Kingsbridge Estuary. This roughly marked the halfway point of the marathon. There were no mile-markers or checkpoints, so we only had our GPS watches to go by.

Sitting between us and the remaining 13 miles of the run was a wide, fast-flowing estuary. There can't be too many marathons that require you to catch a ferry at the halfway point. As the sun was out, the ferry was busy shuttling locals and holidaymakers to and from Salcombe and it was 15 minutes before we got a space on the boat. Not that we were complaining. Standing in the sun, people-watching and taking in the view, it was a very welcome interlude.

I had caught this ferry a few weeks previously, midway through a bike ride with my friend Nick. It was one of the rare occasions I was using my cleated pedals. Climbing from the wooden dock down onto the boat carrying my bike and wearing cycling shoes was a little precarious, but we both boarded the ferry successfully. When we reached the other side, we carried our bikes up the steep steps onto Salcombe's main shopping street. We reached the top and Nick pedalled off up the road. I had just unwrapped a cereal bar so stuffed the whole thing into my mouth, clipped in, and went to pedal after him.

I had been in a big gear as I freewheeled down the hill on the other side of the estuary, and I was still in this big gear as I tried to pedal up the steep street. With both feet clipped in and neither able to move anywhere, I was too slow to unclip, and my bike toppled sideways. I slammed down hard onto the road. I instinctively burst out laughing to hide my embarrassment and then started shouting after Nick to alert him to the fact I had taken a tumble.

With my mouth still full of cereal bar and my body convulsing from laughter, I looked an alarming sight to the handful of shoppers who were out in Salcombe that morning.

'Nwick! Nwick!' I spluttered.

Directly in front of where I fell, three shirtless workmen with high-vis vests were strolling down the street. They rushed over to me, assuming that I was suffering a stroke or seizure. I swallowed the cereal bar and composed myself enough to tell them I was absolutely fine and just terrible at cycling.

'What happened to you?' said Nick when I eventually caught him up.

'Oh, nothing,' I said. 'I was just adjusting my helmet.'

It was an exhilarating feeling for Rachel and me to sit and take the weight off our feet for five minutes on the ferry's hard wooden benches. But even after such a short time, it was a genuine struggle to stand up again once we reached Salcombe. It was at this point I realised why I had never sat down in the middle of a marathon.

Rachel's mood changed dramatically after the ferry crossing. It was as though the act of sitting down on those benches had triggered her brain to send a subconscious message to her body, telling it that the race was over, and she didn't have to run any further. The ragey Rachel I had watched during her final miles in Edinburgh had made a return. The novelty of trail running had well and truly worn off.

From Salcombe, we ran slowly up and down through the bays of North Sands and South Sands, passing smiling couples and families enjoying the beautiful spring day. The section of coast path between South Sands and the dramatically jagged peninsula of Sharp Tor is a popular route for walkers from Salcombe, as it is fairly well-surfaced, and the gradient is forgiving. I enjoyed being around other people for a while. Rachel didn't want to be around anyone. Most walkers turn back once they reach Sharp Tor as the path beyond becomes steeper, narrower and rockier. With the path to ourselves once again, we descended with the enticing waters of Starehole Bay below us. This small cove was the final resting place of Herzogin Ceciliee – a four-mast German ship that hit rocks here in 1936 and later sank. The wreck remains on the seabed just offshore and is a popular dive site.

Rachel had muttered no more than a couple of words since the ferry. Each time I tried to start a conversation, she made it clear with a grunt or a shrug that she wasn't interested in talking. I kept quiet and hoped things would improve, otherwise it was going to be a particularly long and gruelling 11 miles.

Because of the incredible visibility, we could see a tiny island on the horizon, set apart from the mainland (as islands tend to be). It looked like it was hundreds of miles away, and certainly too far to run to. Burgh Island sits about half a mile out to sea from Bantham where our race would finish, and with the absence of any other visible islands along the coast, Rachel made the logical assumption the island we could see must be Burgh Island. I could feel her heart sink as she gazed at the microscopic speck in the distance.

'There's no way we can run there,' she said.

'It does look a very long way. I'm sure Burgh Island is closer than that. We've only got about nine miles to go.'

'Then why can't we see it?'

'I don't know,' I said, feeling demoralised for the first time that day.

The steep descent down to Soar Mill Cove and then up the other side towards Bolberry Down brought Rachel to a standstill. She stood halfway up the sheer hill with her hands on her hips and a glazed expression on her face. She was done. Unfortunately, this section of coast path is so remote, and so far from the nearest road, it is not the sort of place you can just decide to end a run.

'What do you want to do?' I asked.

'I don't know. I can't go on.'

'Well, the only way out of here without running or walking would be to call the air ambulance.'

'Well, I can hardly call the air ambulance because I feel a bit tired, can I?'

'No, I think we're going to have to keep going. At least until we get to Hope Cove. It's not too far. We can always call it a day there.'

The village of Hope Cove was about three miles away, and once we got there, we would only be about four miles from Bantham. I felt confident that if I could persuade Rachel to get to Hope Cove, we would then both be able to finish the race together. She reluctantly agreed to continue.

Despite finding it really tough, Rachel was determined to try and complete the event and not be marked down as DNF (Did Not Finish). Although, considering the relaxed nature of the event, she could probably have been airlifted to Bantham and still be marked down as a finisher.

As we crested the top of the path out of Soar Mill Cove and began slowly trudging along a nice smooth section of coast path alongside Bolberry Down, there in front of us – well, not directly in front of us, still a good seven miles away – was Burgh Island. It was hidden by the headland and tucked closer into shore than we realised. It looked easily reachable. And our finish line at Bantham was even closer than the island. The island we had seen in the distance turned out to be The Great Mew Stone off the coast from Plymouth – a further 25 miles away.

Rachel's mood changed instantly. Her head came up, her shoulders went back, she broke into a light jog, and this strange smile-like thing spread across her face for the first time this side of the estuary.

'Oh, Burgh Island, am I glad to see you!' she said.

There was a lovely long descent through fields into Hope Cove where the path hugs the coastline around the peninsula of Bolt Tail. There is also an alternative path that cuts the corner, saving a distance of about half a mile. We could see a runner ahead of us doing just that, and it was tempting to follow naively behind. But I knew without Bolt

Tail, our distance was unlikely to be a full marathon, so we begrudgingly clung to the coast.

'Those runners that cut the corner are only cheating themselves,' I said.

'Alright, you can stop saying that, George.'

Another feed station greeted us in Hope Cove, kindly manned by Dildo Baggins. Dildo was a regular Hasher (obviously) and had been due to take part in this year's marathon but had suffered a heart attack just days before. He had still wanted to take part, but eventually heeded his doctor's advice and agreed to rest. His resting involved manning a feed station for the entire day.

After a ten-minute chat and banquet, we thanked Dildo Baggins and began the last push to the finish. We were full of food and full of enthusiasm, knowing we now had a relatively straightforward four miles to go.

We had been running for less than five minutes through the village of Hope Cove when we met a group of people in suits and dresses descending some steps from the church to our right. It was a wedding party. They were all heading along the path in the same direction as us. We stopped and waited for the remaining guests to come down the steps and then shuffled along behind. There was a hotel a hundred metres further along, so we assumed they were heading there for the reception. The crowd then came to a standstill, with about a hundred wedding guests now squashed into the narrow pathway below the hotel.

I climbed onto a low wall and looked over the heads to

the front of the line where I could make out the bridal party.

'Can you see anything?' asked Rachel. 'What's the holdup?'

'Yes. It... er... it looks like they are taking the wedding photos.'

'Seriously?'

'Yes, the photographer is getting the families into groups. It looks like we might be here for some time.'

'Ha! Brilliant! What sort of marathon involves being delayed by a wedding?'

'A Devon one.'

We had been in Hope Cove a couple of weeks earlier, meeting up with my friend Damo (who claims his grandma invented banoffee pie) and his family who were holidaying down in Devon. When I told them about our upcoming Salcombe marathon passing through Hope Cove, this was not quite what I envisaged.

Some of the runners behind caught us up and asked what the delay was. Two of the grumpy and more serious marathoners chuffed, stared at their watches, and then chuffed again, wondering how a couple could dare to get married while they were trying to go for a run. The rest of us welcomed the break and chatted and laughed at the bizarreness of it for almost 15 minutes until the guests slowly filed through to the hotel. The bride and groom were still having some couple shots with the ocean views behind as we passed.

'Congratulations!' we shouted.

If we had left the feed station just thirty seconds earlier; if I had had one less Party Ring; if I had not pointlessly untied and retied my shoelaces, we would have reached the church steps before the bride and groom emerged and would be 15 minutes further along the route. But being delayed by a wedding party near the end of a marathon was a lovely unique experience and something that is unlikely to happen in any other race we ever take part in. And I bloody well needed that extra Party Ring.

We were joined for the final four miles from Hope Cove to Bantham by a runner named Sarah. It was lovely to meet a fellow human with a normal name. Sarah was staying in Salcombe on holiday with her in-laws and her young baby. She had been a runner previously but had only recently taken it up again after having her baby. This was her first ever marathon.

'Wow, this is a tough marathon to do as your first,' said Rachel. 'I thought I was mad doing it as my second.' 'I know. I haven't done as much training as I hoped, so I thought an off-road marathon would be a good one to do because I don't have to worry about getting a fast time.'

'Have you enjoyed it?' I asked. 'You look like you are doing really well.'

'I've loved it. It's been really tough, but such a great way to spend the day. And with a young baby at home, it's nice to have a bit of peace and quiet. That sounds really mean, doesn't it?'

'No!' laughed Rachel. 'It doesn't sound mean at all. We have three kids. That's why we do so much running.'

'It's really lovely that you both run together.'

'Yeah, it is,' said Rachel. 'Most of the time.'

'As long as I don't talk too much,' I added. 'About an hour ago, I thought Rachel was going to strangle me or push me off the cliff.'

'I sometimes feel like doing that to my husband,' said Sarah.

'Is your husband a runner?' asked Rachel.

'Yes, but we don't ever run together. He's too quick for me.'

'George is too quick for me, too.'

'I'm not. Well, I used to be, but she'll soon be quicker than me.'

I had completely taken for granted the fact that I was out running a marathon with my wife. Running is often used as an escape, and I knew it was unlikely Rachel would want to run with me regularly. But I felt very fortunate that we were even able to consider running a marathon together.

We descended the last hill into the car park behind Bantham beach and ran towards the finish line. I say finish line, it was actually just a bearded marshal standing next to his car.

'Well done, all of you,' he said. 'Did you enjoy it?'

I looked at Rachel.

'Yes, I loved it. Thank you,' she said.

'That's great to hear. What time would you like me to put down for you?'

'What do you mean?'

'Well, some runners stop their watches when they get the ferry or at feed stations. It's entirely up to you. What time would you like?'

Rachel and I hadn't stopped our watches for the ferry crossing, feed stations or the holdup with the wedding party. They were all part of our run.

'Err... 5 hours 40 minutes please.'

'Great. Well done. Here is your medal.'

I'm not going to lie. The medal was a huge disappointment. It wasn't a medal; it was a badge. A fabric badge, like the kind you get when you swim 100m as a child or sell lots of cookies as a cub scout.

Another lady who finished just behind us gave a time of 5 hours 2 minutes. She started ahead of us, finished behind us, but still recorded a time 40 minutes quicker. We also saw her cut off half a mile at Bolt Tail, but we decided not to point that out.

'She's only cheating herself,' I said.

Rachel rolled her eyes again.

'We ran all that way for this?' laughed Rachel, looking at her crappy badge as we walked towards our car.

'I'll attach some ribbon to it and at least you can then hang it with your other medals.'

There was something very apt about the badge, though. It was certainly in keeping with the understated nature of the event. It would have been inappropriate to be presented with a large shiny medal for what must be one of the most un-glitzy running events out there.

What it lacked in bling, the Salcombe Coastal Marathon made up for in hills. With 4,880ft of climbing, it was certainly tough. And with the added complications of ferries and wedding parties thrown into the mix, it was very slow. But it was also a tremendous amount of fun, and as happy as I was for finishing the run, I was prouder of the fact that Rachel and I had completed it together. And not killed each other.

'Oh bollocks,' said Rachel.

'What's wrong?'

'My watch only says 25.9 miles. What does yours say?'

'26 exactly. The course must be a bit short. Probably because of all that erosion. Oh well.'

'We can't finish short. Come on, let's run around the car park.'

'But we've already finished the race. We ran all the extra bits and could not have made that run any longer. It's not cheating to stop now.'

'George, we will only be cheating ourselves!'

Now it was my turn to roll my eyes. But I knew she was right.

'I'm not uploading this to Strava if it's 0.3 miles short,'

she said.

And with that, she began trudging around the car park. I followed on behind.

My watch ticked over 26.2 just as we passed the car for the second time, and Rachel stubbornly continued for another minute until hers had done the same.

THREE

A year earlier, I had surgery to remove a tumour growing inside my spinal cord. While lying in the hospital bed, I had an idea to sign up for an Ironman triathlon: a 2.4-mile open water swim, a 112-mile bike ride, and a 26.2-mile run. I couldn't swim more than a length of front crawl, I had never ridden a proper road bike before, and I had not run further than 10k in 18 months.

I didn't know if I would complete the Ironman (check out my book *Operation Ironman* to find out if I did). But I knew that it could provide me with a greater incentive to get stronger – both physically and mentally – than if I didn't try.

Swimming was my nemesis throughout my Ironman training. In fact, it had been my nemesis since I was a child, when I spent what felt like most of my childhood trapped in the same swimming group – Stroke Development 4 – while my younger sister quickly progressed up through the ranks.

To undertake the Ironman swim, I had an intensive few months trying to develop my stroke (and find my core). Despite lessons, and countless hours of YouTube videos,

I never gelled with swimming.

During my training, I completed the Plymouth Breakwater swim, where a boat dumped swimmers 2.2 miles out to sea, and then we had to swim back to shore. I also survived the 2.4-mile swim leg of my Ironman in a river in Vichy, France. So there was no doubt that I had got a lot better at swimming. But I still wasn't very good at it. And more importantly, I didn't enjoy it.

But I so wanted to. I would see swimmers return to the beach from long sea swims, grinning from ear to ear. I wanted to be like them.

I didn't have the bravery or willpower to force myself to go for a long open water swim on my own, so knew that the only way to get me to swim any significant distance would be as part of an organised event.

The Dart 10k had been on my radar for a few years. Established in 2009, it was the UK's first 10k swimming event, and has gained a reputation as being one of the most popular swims in the country.

The event follows the River Dart from the town of Totnes towards Dartmouth, ending on the banks of the river in the picturesque village of Dittisham (pronounced Dit-sum by the locals).

'I thought you hated swimming,' said Rachel, after I told her I was considering signing up.

'I do. But I want to like it.'

'And swimming 10k will make you like it?'

'I don't know. There's only one way to find out.'

I paid my entry fee and planned to use the Dart 10k as an incentive to finally become confident with my swimming ability. Over the following months I would train hard, spend hours on dedicated training drills in the pool, combined with regular long open water sessions to build up my stamina and confidence.

At least, that was the plan.

FOUR

I shot myself in the foot by entering Rachel into the Edinburgh Marathon as a surprise Christmas present the previous year. At the time, she felt shocked and a little annoyed. But despite hitting some pretty dark places towards the end of her first marathon, it was clear she wanted to do another. I felt she might almost be disappointed if I didn't sign her up for a marathon as a present the following Christmas. And a marathon weekend away somewhere together also meant that I got to enjoy her Christmas present too.

So, I entered us both into the Rome Marathon. Friends thought it was odd that we would go all the way to Italy to run a marathon.

'You know you can go to Rome and not run a marathon?' they would say.

'That's true, but it would be harder to convince the grandparents to babysit without the marathon. Plus, running 26.2 miles around a city is a pretty effective sightseeing tour.'

Rachel's training had been going really well, but in the weeks leading up to the race she started getting a severe pain in her leg. I was never quite sure which part of her leg was causing the problem, as it seemed to change on a regular basis.

'How's your knee?' I would ask.

'My knee is fine now, but this bit above my ankle really hurts.'

'How's the bit above your ankle?' I would ask the next day.

'Why are you asking about my ankle? It's my knee that's been stopping me from running.'

'I... but... you... oh.'

The following day I would ask, 'How's your knee?'

'My knee doesn't hurt. It's that muscle just below my hip at the top of my leg that hurts.'

I stopped asking after a while as it became too confusing. I didn't dare mention the fact that her legs probably hurt from the 50 miles a week she had been running in preparation. I know my body would hurt all over if I ran 50 miles a week.

To give herself the best shot of being able to take part in Rome, Rachel abstained from running completely in the five weeks before the marathon, had a couple of sessions of physiotherapy, and hoped she would recover in time.

'You'll be fine,' I kept saying. 'I'm sure it's nothing to worry about.'

'But I will have lost all my fitness! I haven't been running for FIVE WEEKS!'

'You won't lose your fitness. You're just doing an

extreme version of tapering.'

As the marathon approached, Rachel's frustration intensified. The day before we were due to fly to Rome she declared:

'I'm DEFINITELY not going to be able to run the marathon.'

'Yes, you are. You'll be fine.'

'YOU DON'T UNDERSTAND!' she shouted. 'My legs hurt now and I'm not even moving. I CAN BARELY EVEN STAND! How am I supposed to run a marathon?'

But I did understand.

I understood exactly how she was feeling. It's not that I thought Rachel was being a drama queen. She was just clearly suffering from a textbook case of pre-marathon paranoia. Or 'maranoia', to give it its official title. As well as fearing that you are going to get ill or injured in the build-up to the race, maranoia causes every little niggle or pain to intensify so that it feels like it's some sort of serious debilitating injury. I obviously didn't tell Rachel this. If I had told her she was being a hypochondriac and suffering from maranoia then I think I would have ended up with a serious debilitating injury of my own.

'I'm sorry. I didn't realise it was that bad,' I said. 'Well, look at it this way, if you aren't able to run, then you still get to have a nice weekend in Rome anyway.'

Rachel considered this for a moment and then smiled for the first time in days.

'That's true,' she said. 'That doesn't sound so bad

actually.'

'It sounds amazing. I think I might have to invent an injury as well.'

'INVENT AN INJURY? WHAT ARE YOU SAYING? ARE YOU IMPLYING I'M MAKING IT UP?' she screamed.

'Oops... no, of course not. That came out wrong.'

At 6am the following morning, we flew to Rome.

Marathon registrations are a huge ball ache. I understand it is how the organisers make a sizeable chunk of their money, with brands and manufacturers paying to get their products in front of their target market. But attending these expos is compulsory for runners to collect their numbers and timing chips, and this usually cannot be done on the morning of the marathon. The expo is never situated in a convenient place in the middle of the city, near to the race start, or a major transport hub. It is invariably in some big conference centre in the arse-end-of-nowhere. Rome's expo was no exception.

Getting there is always an endurance event in itself, and even if you have no interest in looking at the stalls, they cleverly place the exit at the far end, so that you have to walk past every single exhibitor before you are allowed to leave.

There are exhibitors selling the latest in sports energy drinks and nutrition, representatives from other international city marathons, and then many stalls selling running equipment. Particularly trainers. And these stands are always swarming with customers. It confuses me when I see these stalls so busy, as though the day before a marathon, runners have been aimlessly wandering through the expo when they've suddenly had the realisation, 'what a good idea, maybe I should buy some trainers!'

Because of our early flight, there were no queues when we arrived and we raced through the aisles in record time, politely ignoring all the brand representatives trying to convince us to buy their wares. We collected our race numbers – and a very nice blue souvenir t-shirt – and were back out on the street in less than twenty minutes. High fiving each other, we felt smug about the ease with which we had navigated the expo. We crossed the road and began walking to the subway station as hordes of people walked towards us. We had timed our visit perfectly to beat the masses.

'Why do all those other runners have Rome Marathon backpacks,' said Rachel, pointing to a group of people all walking in the same direction as us.

'I don't know. They must have all bought them, I guess.'

'I doubt they would have all bought the same backpack,' she said. 'Look, that group ahead all have them too.'

'Do you think they are freebies that we were supposed to pick up?'

'I don't know. Do you think we should go back?'

'All the way through the expo again?'

'Well, yes. If it means we get our free backpack.'

The backpacks did look very nice. They weren't your usual cheap, disposable plastic goody bag. They were actual backpacks, with pockets, zips and everything.

'But what if we go all the way back and find out they are not free?' I said.

'Let's ask someone. What's Italian for 'did you have to pay for your backpack?''

'I don't know. Quanto Euro por the rucksackio?'

'No, George. I don't think that's it. Look, that guy looks British.'

A man was standing next to us, staring in bewilderment at a map.

'Excuse me. Did you get the backpack for free?'

'Yeah, they are free if you're running the marathon.'

'Where did you get it from?'

'At a stand next to the registration desk. You can't miss it.'

'Oh, ok, thanks. We did.'

We joined the throngs of people and made our way back to the Expo where there was now a sizable queue to get in. We eventually got back into the building, collected our backpacks, weaved our way through the myriad of exhibition rooms and vendors and were back outside 40 minutes after we last stood there smugly.

'Oh well. It was nice to see all of those exhibition stands for a second time. Just to be sure we didn't want to buy any of it,' said Rachel.

'It was definitely worth going back. If we hadn't got our

free backpacks, my weekend would have been ruined.'

A little later than hoped, but still before midday, we made it into the centre of Rome. We were staying in a fantastic apartment on the fourth floor of an old townhouse, on a street just a stone's throw from the Colosseum. Providing you are exceptional at throwing.

We dumped our bags and headed out to explore the city. We would be in Rome for just two days, and one of those would be taken up with the slight matter of running a marathon.

Within minutes of leaving our apartment, we were approached by a large man wearing a tiny tutu, a tight white top trimmed with red hearts straining to contain his bulging stomach, and a pair of wings. He had a big blond curly wig and was clutching a toy bow and arrow. Even with my extremely limited knowledge of mythology, it was clear he was Cupid. Or at least pretending to be. We smiled at him. He smiled back.

'Photo?' he asked.

'No, thank you,' I said. 'But you look belissimo!'

'Photo? English? You take photo!'

He came and stood next to us and put his arm around me.

'No, thank you. We don't have any money.'

'No money. It's ok. Photo. I like you,' he said.

I looked at Rachel. She shrugged.

'Ok, fine,' I said, retrieving my phone from my pocket.

I put my arm around him, took a quick selfie, shook his hand, and then Rachel and I tried to walk off.

'Five euro,' he said.

'What? No! You said no money. I didn't even want a photo with you.'

'Five euro! Photo five euro!'

'I'm not giving you five euros.'

'5 EURO!' he demanded, clutching his bow and arrow slightly more menacingly.

If it had been a proper bow and arrow, I would have handed over everything I owned. As it was, his arrows were tipped with red suckers, and we were in the middle of a busy tourist street. I didn't feel too intimidated.

'5 EURO!' he shouted.

'He does look good,' whispered Rachel.

'Yeah, but not five euros good!' I said, before reluctantly reaching into my pocket and passing him one euro as a gesture of goodwill. I conceded he had made an effort.

'5 EURO!' he said again.

'No, Cupid, you can have ONE euro. Now off you fly!'

We hurried quickly up the road and he sulked off in the other direction. Within seconds he had latched onto another couple who had foolishly smiled at him too.

Cupid probably made a tidy income strolling around Rome in his tutu and wings and lived in a marble palace on the outskirts of the city. To be honest, I was a little envious.

We spent the day wandering the streets of Rome,

soaking up as much as we could during our brief visit. Rome spoiled us for choice in every direction we looked. As it was marathon weekend, the city had swelled by tens of thousands of runners plus their friends and family, so it was busier than a usual weekend in April. Queues for the Colosseum were endless, so we decided to get a pizza and beer at an outdoor café and enjoy the Colosseum from a distance instead.

We walked the perimeter of the Roman Forum, which houses the ruins of many of ancient Rome's most important government buildings. It's a vast and spectacular site, and we accidentally photobombed many bridal photoshoots that were using it as a backdrop. We walked around Palatine Hill, believed to be the oldest part of the city and now home to an open-air museum. We stood and marvelled at the Altar of the Fatherland, one of the biggest buildings I have ever seen, constructed to honour Vittorio Emanuele II, the first king to unify Italy.

Rome is a relatively compact city, with most of the main sights within walking distance of each other, but we covered a lot of ground in those first few hours. Since landing in Rome earlier that morning, Rachel had mentioned nothing about the pain in her knee, or was it her ankle, or maybe hip, that had meant she could BARELY EVEN STAND the previous day. I kept quiet and hoped that she was on the mend.

Mid-afternoon, we stumbled upon The Pantheon. The Pantheon – one of Rome's best-known landmarks – began life as a Roman temple but has been a Roman Catholic church for several hundred years. The long queue stretched into the Piazza della Rotonda, but it seemed to be moving quickly, so we joined it and the vastness of the Pantheon soon swallowed us all up.

The Pantheon was built in about 120AD and its dominant feature is its enormous domed roof. Nearly 2,000 years after it was built, it remains the largest unreinforced concrete dome in the world. Staggeringly, it is still in near perfect condition. In the centre of the dome sits a big hole. This oculus – to give it its official name – was not the result of some lazy builders leaving the job unfinished, but a clever design to allow light to flood the inside of the building. Rain also has a tendency to flood into the building, but those ingenious Romans engineered a sophisticated drainage system using a series of almost invisible holes in the floor. It is a truly magical building, and, despite the number of people, felt strangely uncrowded and serene.

From the Pantheon, we strolled along the river Tiber and crossed the Ponte Sant'Angelo bridge into Vatican City: the world's smallest sovereign state, and home to the Pope. The queues to St Peter's Basilica looked longer than the Rome marathon, so we admired it from the outside and headed back across the river for a coffee.

It was late afternoon when we sat at a small café on a quiet back street. Right across the square from us was the church of Santa Maria Maddalena. It is fairly inconspicuous from the outside, as it is attached to buildings on either side, so almost looks like a mid-terrace house – albeit a beautiful, huge and ornate mid-terrace house. The church took 70 years to build and was completed in 1699, although there had been a church on the site for over a hundred years before that. But by Rome's standards, even the former church could be considered a new build. The door was open and there were a couple of tourists exiting, so we poked our heads through the door.

The moment we crossed the threshold we realised we had discovered something special. When I say discovered, I mean we had visited something that wasn't in our guidebook. It was clear from the inside why it had taken so long to build. I'm not very knowledgeable about architecture, so nothing I write could do it justice. Wikipedia defines the interior of Santa Maria Maddalena as 'architecturally complex', which is even more of a cop-out. But the structure was not even the most impressive thing about the church. Almost every inch of the ceiling, walls and pillars were covered in paintings; incredible frescoes adorned every available surface. It was genuinely breath-taking.

In any other city on earth, the Santa Maria Maddalena church would be the top visitor attraction. People would flock from all over the world to see it. It would receive record star ratings on TripAdvisor. In Rome, it is just a normal church hidden away in a mid-terrace building on a side street. It didn't even get a mention in our guidebook.

We had walked over ten miles, and there was still no mention from Rachel about her leg/ankle/knee/hip. Walking that sort of distance – especially with an injured leg/ankle/knee/hip – was perhaps not the best preparation the day before a marathon, but we both wanted to make the most of our 48 hours in Rome.

The evening before Rachel's first marathon in Edinburgh, I had gone out to buy food from the supermarket and came home with a margarita pizza and some instant rice, which were both considered 'too risky' for Rachel's sensitive stomach. I made a second trip and then cooked her a bowl of plain pasta. It was one thing to insist on eating plain pasta when I was doing the cooking but ordering plain pasta in an Italian restaurant... in Rome, is bordering on criminal.

And that is exactly what Rachel did.

The waiter looked at her as if she had directly insulted his family. I thought I better show willing, so ordered beef carpaccio and pasta arrabbiata. Ordering the spicy arrabbiata the night before a marathon was a decision that very nearly backfired the next day, in a quite literal way.

The waiter chuffed again when we declined dessert. Rachel was saving gelato as a reward for finishing the marathon.

'You know we can have gelato before AND after,' I had argued.

'You can if you want, but I'm going to look forward to

mine after.'

'So, that means you are definitely running tomorrow? You're all cured?'

'I am NOT cured. It's still very sore, but I'm going to see how it goes.'

'That's great that you are going to run. We will take it very easy and hopefully the pain in your knee?... ankle?... hip?... will be ok,' I said, hesitantly.

'It's my foot. I told you it was my foot.'

'Sorry, of course. I meant foot.'

We were staying only a few minutes' walk from the start of the marathon, which meant that we were inevitably late. By the time we arrived, they had closed off the starting pens for the different estimated finishing time groups and they lumped together all stragglers in one mass at the back.

The first thing that struck me about the runners at the start of the Rome Marathon was that they were predominantly men. Rachel seemed to be very much in the minority by a ratio of at least 5 to 1. I checked the breakdown of the results later (because that's the sort of cool thing I do in my spare time) and discovered that out of 13,881 runners, only 2,778 were female. According to a 2018 worldwide study into marathon statistics (conducted by Jens Jakob Andersen and Vania Nikolova – both bigger geeks than me), Italy has one of the most unequal gender balances for marathons (15% female) out of all 30 countries studied, with only Spain, Portugal, Korea,

Slovenia, Switzerland, and India faring worse. The USA topped the chart with an impressive 43%, and the UK was a little behind in fourth (33%).

But female participation in running events across all distances has seen a dramatic rise in the last few decades. In 1986, less than 20% of participants in running events were female. By 2018, this number had leapt to just above 50%, with an incredible 60% of 5k runners being female. This was why the gender split at the start of the Rome Marathon seemed so noticeable.

'How are you feeling?' I asked Rachel. 'Is the... foot... feeling any better today?'

'I don't know. We will see how it goes. I might not make it all the way round, but I'll keep up with you for as long as I can.'

'I don't think there will be any danger of not keeping up with me. It's much more likely to be the other way round.'

The starting horn sounded, there was a collective cheer from the runners and spectators, and we were off.

The marathon begins and ends on the Via dei Fori Imperiali – the imposing wide road that runs through the centre of Rome from the Colosseum to the Piazza Venezia, with parts of the ruined Roman Forum on either side. It is a spectacular start for a marathon. At the time, I was ignorant of the fact that this road was built by Mussolini, and its construction involved the demolition of hundreds of houses, several churches and a monastery, which does taint it slightly.

The wide four-lane highway soon funnelled into one of the smaller cobbled streets that winds its way through the old part of the city. We were forced to walk a short section as runners created a bottleneck. There was a fair amount of shouting and theatrical arm waving going on from the Italians because of the slow pace.

'Mamma Mia!' I said to Rachel, in a poor Italian accent. She rolled her eyes at me. We were both quite pleased to have an excuse to walk for a couple of minutes and soak up the atmosphere. We could hardly complain about the thousands of runners backed up ahead of us, as it was our own fault for being late to the start.

The organisers of the Rome Marathon have done a brilliant job of showcasing most of Rome's famous sights during the run. This did mean some sections were on the narrow streets, but it is a sacrifice well worth making. Another concern had been the cobbles. Large sections of the route run along the old cobbled streets and Rachel and I had read warnings and reviews of how challenging they are. We envisaged miles and miles of uneven terrain, having to watch our footing constantly, but it turns out those Romans were actually pretty good at engineering (who'd have thought?) and the cobbles posed no problem whatsoever.

The first few miles of the marathon wound their way around the streets in the centre of Rome, the crowds lined behind the barriers, several deep on either side. Many others stood clapping at their windows or balconies high above us.

For some locals, however, the marathon was just an enormous inconvenience. On a couple of occasions, we were running through a long narrow section, shoulder to shoulder with other runners, and then a man or woman would stride out between a gap in the barriers, completely oblivious to the thousands of runners, and saunter across the marathon course as though we weren't even there. Rachel and I would smile politely and dodge around these pedestrians. But the Italian runners were not so forgiving. They would begin shouting abuse at the pedestrian, before a full-on argument ensued, with both runner and pedestrian comically waving their arms and yelling at each other, until either the runner or pedestrian was out of sight.

'Mamma Mia!! I said to Rachel.

'Alright, George. You can stop saying that now. It's not funny and I think you need to learn some more Italian.'

The middle section of the marathon looped out into the outskirts of Rome, through residential streets, industrial estates and commercial districts. These miles are obviously not as picturesque as the famous sights of Rome's centre, but during those quieter miles in the outskirts, it was reassuring to see that a city as glorious as Rome, like all other cities, also has its shit bits.

We crossed the bridge into Vatican City again, and

directly past St Peter's Basilica, and were a little disappointed not to see the pope standing outside high-fiving runners as we passed. In March 2019, Pope Francis was filmed refusing to shake the hands of worshippers or letting them kiss the papal ring. Defying centuries of catholic tradition, many were shocked and furious by this behaviour. This was almost a year before the Covid-19 pandemic, but is it possible Pope Francis had received some premonition or warning from above? Regardless, it is unlikely that high-fiving sweaty runners was his thing.

Rachel showed no signs of injury. Her knee, sorry, foot, which two days previously had made standing in our kitchen almost physically impossible, was now incredibly cured. It was a miracle! It must have been our visit to the Vatican the day before.

It was unseasonably hot for April, but there were patches of shade to be found running down the edges of the tree-lined avenues. It was a beautiful day for a 26.2-mile sightseeing tour. We were both thoroughly enjoying ourselves.

For a city built on seven hills, Rome is remarkably flat. The seven hills thing is a lie. There are not seven hills in Rome. There are about four or five humps. Nothing that you could really call a hill. I think perhaps the Romans weren't very fond of hills.

The Romans invaded Britain in AD 50-55 and took over many parts of the country. However, very little evidence of the Romans has ever been found west of Exeter in Devon. It is now obvious to me it was because of the hills. If they thought Rome was hilly, imagine how they felt when they reached Britain's West Country. I think they probably ventured through Devon, had a quick peek at Cornwall, and thought 'nah, fuck that', before heading back up country.

To be fair, I nearly did the same thing after my first run when we moved to Devon. But I'm glad I persisted. After living there for eight years, I still don't find running or cycling up hills any easier, but it has made me re-establish my definitions of what constitutes a 'hill'. And not one of Rome's supposed seven makes the cut.

By 18 miles I was beginning to flag. My legs were getting a little wobbly and our pace had slowed considerably because of me. I was taking energy gels regularly, but their effect was short-lived. I was seeking shade wherever I could, blaming the sun and the energy gels for my fatigue, when, in truth, it was just that, despite her enforced five-week taper, I wasn't as fit as Rachel and was struggling to keep up. I had known for a while that this moment would come. Part of me felt disheartened that I had slipped behind in fitness and was now the weaker runner. The other part of me was mightily impressed that Rachel had come so far in such a short time. I tried to persuade her to go ahead, but she insisted she wanted us to run together. After we had completed 20 miles, I got a second wind knowing that the end was nearing, and I would soon be allowed that gelato.

As the route returned to the centre of Rome, it was lovely to once again be distracted by the fine architecture and the energetic supporters.

We gazed in wonder at what we thought was the Trevi Fountain, only to later discover it was just a fountain. We ogled at what we thought were the famous Spanish Steps, only to later discover they were actually some Italian steps, and some unremarkable Italian steps at that.

Rachel was on a real high. Having convinced herself she would not be able to run, she was grinning from ear to ear in a slightly crazed way. It was contagious, and with a mile to go I encouraged her to pick up the pace and we both ran together down the Via dei Fori Imperiali, with the magnificent view of the Colosseum in front of us.

We crossed the finish line – our second marathon together – in a very respectable time of 4 hours 13 minutes.

'Well done,' I said between gasps as I gave Rachel a hug. 'That was brilliant.'

'I really loved that. Thanks for such an amazing Christmas present.'

'It's incredible that you were able to get around considering you were unable to even stand a couple of days ago. And now you've got a new personal best.'

'Yes, maybe my injury wasn't as bad as I thought.'

'Well, I'm glad your foot has healed.'

'It was my knee!'

As we sat drinking beer and eating gelato after the race, I realised it was exactly a year to the day since I had been lying in a hospital bed recovering from surgery to remove a spinal cord tumour.

I had come a long way in those 12 months. I had completed three marathons, three 100-mile bike rides, a 2.2 mile sea swim, an ultramarathon, and (*SPOILER ALERT*) the small matter of an Ironman. It is fair to say I was well on the road to recovery.

It was a strange feeling to be grateful for having that spinal cord tumour. But I undoubtedly was. I would not have attempted any of the things I had done in the previous year had it not been for that setback to kick-start my desire to get fit. And without that tumour and the events that followed, I knew I would not be sitting drinking beer and eating gelato in Rome.

We woke the next morning with aching bodies and sore heads, which were indications of a successful run and appropriate post-race celebrations. We had to get the train to the airport by midday but left the apartment early and went for breakfast at a nearby café. After breakfast, we walked our tired legs to look at the real Trevi Fountain and the real Spanish Steps that we somehow missed during the run.

The Trevi fountain was phenomenal. It exceeded all expectations in size, opulence and beauty. The Spanish Steps... not so much. They were just some steps with lots of people sitting on them. To be fair, it did look like a delightful place to sit. But in April 2019, they introduced rules banning people from sitting on the Spanish Steps, depriving them of their only redeeming feature. Now they are just some steps.

'Shall we walk to the train station or take the bus?' I asked.

'I don't mind. Is it far? My legs are pretty sore.'

'I don't think it's too far. Maybe half a mile or so?'

'Fine, let's walk.'

It turned out to be closer to two miles, and that included going over the biggest of Rome's humps (definitely not a hill). When we arrived at the train station, Rachel was angry with me for not getting the bus, and the debilitating injury to her foot, knee, hip or ankle had returned.

There was a queue at the ticket office, so I opted to use one of the machines instead. I stuck in my card, selected the airport as the destination, and it gave me an option of available trains.

I clicked the top one, and a warning message appeared on the screen.

THE TRAIN YOU HAVE SELECTED DEPARTS IN LESS THAN 5 MINUTES. ARE YOU SURE YOU WANT TO PROCEED?

I looked at Rachel.

'NO! We don't even know where the platform is. We're not in a major rush. Just pick the next one instead.'

I looked back at the machine. Paused for a second. And then pressed the YES button.

'WHAT ARE YOU DOING? WHY WOULD YOU DO THAT?'

'We will be fine,' I said nonchalantly, as the machine spent another precious minute of our time printing the tickets.

I grabbed them and we sprinted away, before realising we didn't have a clue where we were going. We scanned the departures board and located the platform number, so dashed the length of the station towards where we thought our platform was. I assumed Rachel was behind me, but when I turned and looked back, she was hobbling slowly further back.

'I really hate you,' she said. 'We ran a marathon yesterday!'

'I know. I'm sorry. We'll get there.'

There was a sign where the entrance to the platform was supposed to be saying it was closed and directing us to another set of stairs further down the station. Rachel's hatred escalated. We reached our platform's ticket barrier and staggered onto the train with a couple of seconds to spare.

'See, I told you we would make it!'

'Well done. And what have we achieved? We just have to wait longer at the airport now, and my legs are much more painful than they would have been if we'd caught the later train.'

'But running for the train was quite exciting, wasn't it?' I said.

'No, it wasn't!' she said, but I saw a hint of a smile that suggested maybe she had enjoyed the rush too.

'I promise we won't have to do any more running today, and you can give your knee a rest.'

'IT'S MY HIP!'

FIVE

For the last couple of years, I had been trying to persuade Rachel to take part in a triathlon. She was not in the least bit tempted, but I was still adamant it was something she would enjoy once she experienced it.

'Which part of NO don't you understand? I am NOT doing a triathlon,' she said.

'Why not? We could do one together. Just a short one. You'd love it.'

'No! I am NOT doing one.'

'Why?'

'Well, for a start I can't swim front crawl... and you know how much I hate cycling. I enjoy running, which is why I'm very happy sticking to running events. We've run two marathons together. Isn't that enough? Why do we have to do a triathlon?'

'I just think it would be fun. And anyway, you don't hate cycling. You just hate squeaky brakes and changing gears.'

'Brakes and gears are both quite crucial parts of cycling. I am not doing a triathlon. Please stop asking me. Triathlons are for triathletes.'

I didn't push it any further on that occasion, but I knew – or at least hoped – there would be a time in the not-too-distant future when she would finally succumb.

The South Hams Triathlon (now rebranded as the Dartmouth Triathlon) was a relatively new event in South Devon. They offered two distances – a Sprint and a Super Sprint. The shorter one – The Super Sprint – was comprised of a 400m sea swim, 20k bike and a 2.5k run. It's a distance designed specifically for beginners. I had wanted to sign Rachel up as a surprise Christmas present, but she got wind of it and made it very clear she would divorce me if I did.

I asked my 67-year-old dad if he would be interested in taking part with me instead. He seemed a little shocked by the idea, having never done or even been tempted by a triathlon. But his shock of being asked was only surpassed by my shock of him saying yes. I bought him a place as a Christmas present and with the triathlon in the middle of June the following year, that left him with nearly six months to prepare.

My dad is not a confident swimmer, but he visited the local swimming pool regularly to try and improve his breaststroke. The triathlon swim would take place in the sea, and the thought of swimming 400m (the equivalent of 16 lengths of a swimming pool) in the open water was very daunting for him, as well as for me. I told my dad we would stay together throughout, but less than a week before the triathlon, he decided to pull out of the event. He wasn't feeling confident enough in his swimming abilities, had come down with a bad cold, and was also suffering a few other niggling injuries. I completely understood his decision for withdrawing and felt very guilty for putting unnecessary pressure on him.

Three days before the triathlon, and with Dad's entry going spare, I subtly suggested to Rachel that she take his place.

'Oh, here we go again! You are SO annoying. I told you, I am NOT doing a triathlon.'

'But why not? It's a free place. I contacted the organisers and they said it's fine to change Dad's name to yours. It's the perfect opportunity for you to do a triathlon. You'll love it!'

'Triathlons are for triathletes!'

'No, they aren't. Anyone who completes a triathlon is a triathlete. And you will complete it. It will be a brilliant way to spend a couple of hours. We'll be home before lunch.'

'A couple of hours? Yeah, right! How can we do all that swimming, biking and running, plus all that faffing in between, and it take less than two hours? It will take me all day.'

'It honestly won't. You'll be done in much less than two hours, I promise. It will be less than half the time of one of your marathons. It will take less time than watching a film.'

'I'd much rather watch a film.'

'Ok, bad example.'

'Seriously... all that swimming, biking, running and

faffing will take less than two hours? Even for someone like me who can't swim or cycle?'

'Absolutely. They are fairly short distances of each.'

'Hmmm.'

That 'hmmm' was the most positive comment Rachel had ever made about taking part in a triathlon. And it was all I needed to continue my attempts at persuasion.

'Go on!' I said. 'What's the worst that could happen?'

'Err... where do I start? I could drown. I could crash my bike. I could have a heart attack.'

'You won't drown. There will be lots of people in kayaks watching us during the swim, and I'll stay with you for the entire event. We'll do it together.'

'But I still might crash my bike or have a heart attack?'

'No, you won't. You're very fit with all your running and we'll take it easy on the bike. It'll be fun. I promise.'

'Hmmmmmm.'

This was a slightly longer 'hmm' than before, and for the first time, there was a glimmer of hope that Rachel was warming to the idea of becoming a triathlete.

Later that evening, she agreed to give it a go.

'Do you promise I won't drown?' she said.

'I promise.'

Rachel had not done any open water swimming before or taken part in any sort of cycling event. But she owned a cheap wetsuit, a pair of goggles, a rusty mountain bike, and a pair of trainers. She was good to go.

Signing up for the triathlon at such short notice gave Rachel no time to prepare. But this worked in her favour, as it also gave her little time to worry about the event and over think it. She had no goal of a finishing time (in fact, anything under an entire day would be quick, judging by her expectations), and providing she didn't drown, crash her bike or have a heart attack, it would be considered a successful event.

On the morning of the triathlon, Rachel was surprisingly positive. She had the expected pre-race nerves – as did I – but she was also mildly excited about trying something new. And the fact we were going to do it together allayed some of the fear aspect for both of us.

The event started and finished at Blackpool Sands, a few miles down the coast from Dartmouth. Blackpool Sands – not to be confused with the town of Blackpool in Lancashire – is a beautiful cove beach, which tends to be fairly sheltered, making it an ideal location for a triathlon swim.

We arrived at the Race HQ in plenty of time and took our bike, clothes and shoes to the transition area.

'This feels really weird,' said Rachel, as we hung her clunky mountain bike on the rack.

'Doing a triathlon?'

'Yes. I feel really sick.'

'You'll be fine. Just see it as a day out.'

'A DAY? I thought you said it would only take a couple of hours at the most!'

'Sorry, I meant the whole experience. Yes, it will only take a couple of hours. Just try to see it as an adventure.'

'Are you nervous?'

'Yes, I am a bit. But I'm also looking forward to it.'

During my Ironman, much of the stress and anxiety that I felt about the event was brought on because of the logistics involved; ensuring I had all the correct kit with me, checking everything worked and that it was all in the right place. And then during the race, there was the constant worry of a bike malfunction and that all my admittedly haphazard preparation over the previous four months would come tumbling down in an instant. Before the South Hams Triathlon, I only felt a small fraction of this anxiety. Partly because I had been through it all before so knew more about what to expect. But mostly because it was a smaller and more informal event, and there was not the same level of expectation for us to finish. If either of us had problems with our bikes during the triathlon, or if Rachel decided she really didn't want to continue, we could call the race support or just walk our bikes back to the start and we would still be home in time for lunch. A few days earlier, Rachel didn't even know she was going to be taking part in a triathlon, so the possibility of a Did Not Finish was not a concern for her.

A few friends of ours were taking part in the slightly longer Sprint distance triathlon on the same day. This was comprised of a 750m swim, 20k bike and a 5k run.

Competitors for this event set off 30 minutes before our Super Sprint, so we stood on the beach in our wetsuits watching the earlier racers complete their swims.

Large waves were crashing onto the shore, but this was due to it being a shelving beach. Once you were out past the first break, it looked a little choppy, but the swell was not too gnarly (as the surfers probably say). Sprint distance competitors were required to swim out to a buoy, turn left and continue a couple of hundred metres to another buoy and then back the way they came. Our swim would be the same, but our second buoy was a little closer to the first.

Only 12 minutes after the Sprint competitors entered the water, the first of them was back on the beach. Some of the other swimmers had only just passed the first buoy. We stood and clapped as one by one the 174 competitors emerged from the water. We watched as our friends Darren and Kate – both strong swimmers – emerged looking good. A few minutes later, another friend Sophie rose from the water. 25 minutes had passed and there were still about a dozen swimmers spread out between the buoys. One of them was our good friend Simon. If you've read my book Operation Ironman, this Simon is not the same Simon who became my triathlon guru in Vichy, France. This Simon is a triathlon novice. But he's a great friend and always up for a challenge. Despite only being able to manage a few slow lengths of breaststroke, he decided to give the triathlon a go.

The planned start time of the Super Sprint came and

went, as organisers waited until all the Sprint swimmers were out of the water before allowing us to head en masse into the sea.

A few minutes later, Simon emerged from the water looking a little wobbly on his feet but still smiling. He had been convinced he would be the slowest swimmer by some distance, but there were still another five or six competitors in the water behind him.

We cheered and clapped as he made his way up the beach. Any expectations of doing a heroic Baywatch-style run into transition were kicked in the gutter once swimmers realised that the shelving shingle beach was almost impossible to run up with any sort of style or grace, some resorting to an actual crawl to get up the steeper section.

Moments after the final swimmer came out of the water, our starting whistle sounded, and we began our short dash down the beach and into the waves. As this was a triathlon consisting mostly of first timers, there was no melee of people desperate to get into the water first. In fact, people loitered around on the shore, ushering each other into the water in a very civilised manner.

Rachel and I waded in until we were past the first wave break and then set off at a steady pace towards the first buoy. 10 months earlier I had been the triathlon newbie, extremely under-prepared and naively taking part in an Ironman. Now, swimming alongside Rachel, the nervous first timer, I felt like a veteran.

Rachel was wearing an old wetsuit she had bought from a supermarket years ago to use for body boarding. It was big, thick and restrictive, but was more than adequate for swimming 400m. Rachel had not swum front crawl since she was a child and was possibly worse at it than I had been when I began training for my Ironman. So, we swam mostly breaststroke, as did many of those around us, and we were soon around the first buoy. Despite the waves, the water was beautifully clear, and the sun was out, making it a surprisingly enjoyable swim.

Before we had even reached the first buoy, the lead swimmer was already coming back the other way from the second buoy, finishing his swim in under eight minutes, and over three minutes ahead of the swimmer in second place.

There were only 42 of us in the Super Sprint, so it wasn't difficult for Rachel and me to stay together. We were back on the beach after 13 minutes, and when we later looked at the results, we discovered we had finished 8th and 9th after the swim leg. This is not an illustration of how good at swimming we were. Quite the opposite. It's proof that these beginner triathlons really are open to all abilities.

Our transition was going to be interesting. A week earlier, we had gone swimming as a family to the local pool and I had showered myself, washed the hair of all three children, and helped them all get dry and dressed, before Rachel had even finished her shower.

'There won't be time to wash your hair today,' I said as

we trudged up the beach towards the bike racks.

'I don't need to wash it. Just so long as there's a hairdryer.'

I laughed and then looked at her suspiciously.

'You are joking, right?' I said.

'Of course I am joking! Do we have time to get a hot chocolate from the café, though?'

We were out of our wetsuits, into our trainers, and onto our bikes in 4m 30s, which felt like we had done the slickest transition ever. The first swimmer out of the water, who went on to win the event, completed his transition in 1m 09s. How did he even have time to moisturise?

Rachel had owned her mountain bike for about three years. During those three years, she had ridden a total of about 10 miles, yet the damp and salty Devon air had already made the bike look like it had ridden around the world several times. The bike leg of the South Hams triathlon was 20k (12.4 miles), therefore further than Rachel had cycled in the previous three years combined.

I had borrowed my dad's old road bike for my Ironman but had given it back to him at the beginning of the year so that he could train for this triathlon. I was riding my cyclocross bike that I had bought for my Ironman training. It's basically the size and shape of a road bike, but with thicker tyres and a chunkier frame.

The bike route began with a long slow climb up the hill away from the beach at Blackpool Sands to the village of

Strete. The challenging gradient was made more bearable by the stunning views of the sea down to our left. Towards the top of the hill, the road levelled slightly around a long left-hand bend. I had just completed the swim leg of a triathlon with my wife and was feeling very proud and fortunate. It was something I had been wanting to do for a while but had almost given up hope of.

And then I heard a loud scream from Rachel behind me. I looked back and saw her walking her bike backwards out of a small hedge.

'Shit, are you ok?' I said, pulling over to the side of the road.

'Yes, I'm fine,' she laughed.

'What happened?'

'I don't know. I must have misjudged the corner.'

'How did you crash into the hedge on the inside of the corner?'

'I must have turned too early.'

'We weren't even going fast. The trick is to turn when the road turns, not before. It's much easier if the bike stays on the tarmac.'

'Alright. You think you're some sort of cycling expert now do you, Louis Armstrong?'

'Louis Armstrong?'

'That cycling man who won all those Tour de Frances.'

I nearly choked on a mouthful of the water I was drinking.

'It's Lance Armstrong, not Louis Armstrong. And they

took all those Tour de France wins away from him because he turned out to be a drugs cheat.'

'Well, I think winning the Tour de France on drugs is even more impressive. I can't even stay on the road sober.'

'Are you ok after your little detour?'

'I'm fine, thanks. I'm just going to have a drink. Is that ok? Are we in a rush?'

'Nope. No rush at all. We have... wait for it...' I said, clearing my throat and preparing to put on a deep, gravelly voice, '... all... the time... in the world.'

'Isn't that a song?'

'Yes, it's by...'

'I know, don't tell me... Neil Armstrong!'

'Yes, that's right.,' I groaned. 'Neil Armstrong. Well done.'

The bike leg was an out and back route, and the Sprint distance competitors were already returning towards us. We offered our encouragement to them as we climbed back on our bikes and resumed pedalling.

The roads were still wet after heavy rain the night before, and marshals with flags were stationed at each bend on the long downhill to the beach at Strete Gate, encouraging cyclists to slow down.

At Strete Gate we joined the Slapton Line, which is pretty much the only section of flat road in the whole of south Devon. Flanked on either side by water – the sea to the left and the fresh water of Slapton Ley on the right –

the road continues straight as an arrow for about 2.5 miles. This road gets regularly destroyed in big sea storms and has had countless repairs and rebuilds over the years. Each time they rebuild the road, the local council claim it will be the last time they repair it before they allow nature to take its course. But, thankfully, after each destruction, public pressure and environmental concern about what would happen if the sea broke through to the freshwater has paved the way (excuse the pun) for another rebuild. Which is a relief, because the bike leg of this triathlon would have been a lot more challenging without the road.

One by one, Darren, Kate and Sophie passed us. And then we looked up and unexpectedly saw Simon whizzing along at a cracking speed on his retro road bike. After being one of the last out of the water on the swim, he had made up at least 30 places on his bike.

The 20k bike leg consisted of three uphills, three downhills, and two lengths of the long flat section alongside Slapton Ley. The top of the second hill marked the turnaround point.

Rachel still seemed to be enjoying herself. Each time I looked back to see if she was keeping up with me on the bike, she was right there on my back wheel (not literally). We took it steady around the corners, just in case she took the racing line into the hedge.

'Are you having fun?' I asked tentatively.

'I am.'

'So, are you glad you entered?'

'Ask me at the end. If I'm still alive.'

'You are very dramatic.'

'Well, you never know. You said I wasn't going to crash today.'

'Does that count as a crash? You stayed on your bike and you're not hurt.'

'I think it still counts as a crash. I left the road and went into a hedge.'

Rachel is quite a determined and strong-willed person, but this determination and willpower used to evaporate to nothing when she was on a bike and presented with a hill. This wasn't because she found cycling up hills too much of a challenge; more the thought of cycling up them seemed too daunting. On the few bike rides we had previously done together before having children, she would get off her bike at the mere sight of a hill. She would use any distraction as an excuse: picking blackberries in the hedgerow, looking at a butterfly, tying a shoelace, cleaning her sunglasses. Anything to avoid actually attempting to cycle uphill.

But as we reached the halfway point on the bike leg, there she was, cycling up her second hill of the day.

'Look at you. You're cycling up another hill,' I said.

'I know. Look at me go.'

'Why haven't you stopped to pick blackberries yet?'

'Because it's June. Blackberries won't be in season for a couple more months.'

'And if they were, would you have stopped?'

'It's a triathlon, George. You don't tend to see many triathletes picking blackberries.'

'Ah, so you're admitting you're a triathlete now?'

'I... no... er...'

At the top of the second hill, we circled a mini roundabout in the village of Stokenham and then headed back down to the Slapton Line. It was much harder work on the way back, with the wind now full in our face. We didn't overtake any other cyclists during the whole of the bike leg and a steady stream of others passed us, but we kept up a respectable pace and I was in awe of the fact that – other than her little detour into the hedge – Rachel kept pedalling for the duration.

The final climb up to Strete was a fair slog and Rachel was slowing, but she refused to stop, and we made it to the top where we could almost freewheel the last mile to the transition at Blackpool Sands.

On the final bend, a tight right-hand corner at the bottom of the steepest section, a couple of marshals were frantically waving their flags, getting riders to slow down. A cyclist was lying motionless on the side of the road and was being attended to by race officials. It was a concerning sight and made Rachel feel more justified in her worry, but also allowed her to reconsider that perhaps her little off-road detour had not been too serious after all. We later found out that the cyclist had been taken to hospital, but after some stitches and x-rays, was thankfully discharged without serious injuries.

We finished the bike leg in 1h 3m, which was 20 minutes slower than the quickest cyclist, but there were still plenty of riders slower than us.

We dismounted our bikes and walked them to the transition area.

'How are you feeling?' I asked.

'Good. I'm glad that bit is over. Just the run to go. I like running. I can do running.'

At this point I decided not to warn Rachel that the run leg of a triathlon is not like a normal run. She would find that out for herself soon enough.

We racked our bikes into their designated spots and removed our helmets. Neither of us were wearing cycling shoes, so our transition was pretty speedy.

'Right, are you ready?' I said. 'Only 2.5k of running to go.'

'Yey!' said Rachel, breaking into a light jog. 'OH MY GOD! WHAT HAS HAPPENED TO MY LEGS?'

'Do they feel a bit weird?'

'It feels like I'm still on my bike.'

'Yes, it takes a bit of getting used to.'

'OOOH, I DON'T LIKE THIS AT ALL! It's like when you get off a moving escalator and the ground still feels like it's moving.'

The previous year, the run course of the South Hams

Triathlon had involved a scenic loop up the valley, but this had involved crossing a busy road at the start and end of the run, so organisers had taken the decision to drastically redesign the run route at the last minute. The newly designed route was a bit of a mess. It involved a convoluted tangle of laps of the car park and an adjacent camping field. One minute you would be on gravel, the next sand, and then some muddy grass sections. The path was very narrow, so there was often no room to overtake or be overtaken, and the route had runners coming the other way for a good chunk of it, meaning you had to avoid head-on collisions too. There were even a couple of small barriers that we had to hurdle, making the whole thing feel more like a 2.5k obstacle course. But that wasn't necessarily a bad thing.

'Is this pace alright for you?' I said.

'Er, yeah. I think so. I can't really feel my legs.'

'It's only 2.5k. Let's get it over with.'

Some Super Sprint competitors had completed their run before we even started ours, and there were still many of the Sprint distance runners on the course completing their slightly longer distance.

Rachel and I crossed the finish line together in a time of 1h 34m, which was – as promised – quicker than most films. I gave Rachel a big hug.

'Well done. You were amazing, you triathlete, you. See, I knew you could do it.'

'Thank you. I loved it. Well done you! Well done us!'

Our friends from the Sprint distance were there to greet us, and we congratulated them on their achievements. Kate, one of our friends, had got chatting to the winner of the Super Sprint. He completed the event in an incredible 1 hour 6 minutes and was almost eight minutes ahead of the person in second place. Drew Clark was only 15 years old and had become inspired as an 11 year-old watching the London 2012 Olympics and the heroics of the athletes, and in particular Alistair and Jonny Brownlee winning their gold and bronze medals in the triathlon. A few years after watching the Brownlee brothers, Drew Clark was not only competing in his own triathlons, but comfortably beating the rest of the adult field.

We typed our race number into a computer near the finish line and a printer spat out a ticket with a breakdown of our results and splits.

'Fifth female? What?' said Rachel. 'FIFTH FEMALE? That can't be right.'

'That's awesome. And it says you were FIRST in your age group.'

'Wow! I thought I would be last. What does yours say?'

'I was 11th male. I'm very happy with that. Oh, and I was first in my age group too. There must be some mistake? Surely I can't have been first?'

I checked the results online later and I was indeed first in my age group. It was a very niche group of males aged 35-39 and there were just TWO of us in the category.

There were four in Rachel's age group, but to finish 5th female from a field of 27 in her first triathlon was an impressive feat.

'So, are you going to sign up for another?' I asked.

'No, I don't think so. I mean, it was fun, but I think I only enjoyed it because I didn't have time to worry about it or prepare.'

'I know what you mean. So does that mean I can just randomly sign you up for another triathlon and not tell you about it until the day before?'

'Don't you dare!'

I could understand how Rachel felt. There is something very refreshing about spontaneously agreeing to do something at the last minute. Your expectations are lowered considerably because you haven't prepared, and it becomes a different sort of challenge. If you prepare for something for months, then you are likely to build up various hopes and expectations and maybe the goal of a particular finishing time. This is not necessarily a bad thing, as it's always good to push ourselves. But it's also nice to just set ourselves a challenge and see what happens. That's why these beginner triathlons are such wonderful opportunities. They really are open to anyone. Many of these events use swimming pools for the swim section, and although perhaps not as fun as open water swimming, it takes away a lot of the fear associated with triathlon, and also means there is no need to acquire a wetsuit. The other attraction of pool-based triathlons is that because of the restrictions of the pool size, the start is staggered so only a few swimmers start at a time. This has the benefit of ensuring you never feel like you are last. Often the weaker swimmers will start first, meaning they are out of the pool and onto the bike long before the faster swimmers have even got their toes wet. And you never know, you, like Rachel, might find you enjoy it.

SIX

A week after our triathlon, I received a text message from Daniel and Marta. Daniel and Marta are our super-fit Spanish friends who Mark and I ran with for the final seven miles of my first ultramarathon. It said:

'We iz going to run marathon tomorrow. You wantz to join uz?'

'A marathon? Tomorrow? Where? Count me in!' I replied.

'We don't know. We drop zee kids at zee school and then run zee marathon.'

Daniel and Marta didn't write text messages like this. Their spoken and written English was perfect. I'm just trying (and failing) to give them a bit of Spanish character.

'Ok!' I replied. 'See you in zee morning!'

Daniel had sent the text to a couple of other friends too, and the following morning five of us met at the school gates dressed in our running kits and each carrying a small backpack with water and a few snacks.

Rachel had to go to work, and I felt a little guilty about running a marathon without her. On a school day. But I soon got over it when I saw what glorious weather we had for it.

The five of us ran together out to the South West Coast Path and spent the day meandering up and down the rugged coastline in the sweltering heat, stopping regularly to eat and drink. One of our group – Aimee – could only join us for the first half and left at midday. Four of us remained – Daniel, Marta, a South African friend named Charles, and me. I was the least fit of the four of us, but Daniel, Marta and Charles were happy to go at my pace and we walked up most of the steeper hills. The others took regular energy gels to keep themselves fuelled for the duration, but as I was all out of gels, I had opted for a different kind of nutrition strategy.

'What iz zees you are eating?' asked Daniel as we walked up a steep and rocky path with the waves crashing against the rocks below us.

'Mmmm, chweese swanwich,' I replied.

'Que?'

'I think he said a cheese sandwich,' said Charles.

It's always savoury foods that I crave when running, particularly salty food – presumably because of the salt lost through sweating. A cheddar cheese sandwich (grated cheese tastes SO much better than sliced cheese) with lots of salt and pepper and butter. It tasted incredible. It might prove challenging to eat during a road marathon, but while walking up the steep coast path it was perfect. Like a walking picnic.

'A cheeeeze sandwich? You Ingleesh iz weird,' said Daniel.

'Tell me about it,' said South African Charles.

We had covered almost 18 miles when we reached the bottom of yet another long uphill climb and Daniel, Marta and Charles began a gentle jog up the path. My legs were screaming in agony, and I was desperate to walk, but this path wasn't as steep as many of the others we had climbed. I knew if I started walking this one there would be little chance I would make it up any of the others. I also didn't want to be the one to stop and make the others feel obliged to walk too. I trudged on. A few seconds later, still with a long way to go, I was looking down at my feet when I almost stumbled into Charles who had slowed on the path in front of me. He had slowed behind Marta who has slowed behind Daniel. 'Sorry, guys. I'm just going to walk zeez bit,' said Daniel. 'You go on. I'll catch you up.'

'NO!' we all said, wanting to hug him, delighted to walk again.

I pulled out a bag of crisps from my backpack.

'What are you eating now?' said Marta, chugging down another energy gel.

'Cwisps.'

'Crisps?'

'Yeah, cwisps. Whwant one?'

'No zank you,' she laughed.

Crisps are my weakness. It doesn't matter how full I am, or how many crisps are placed in front of me, I have never been in a situation in my life where I have not wanted to eat more crisps. They are, without a doubt, the greatest food on the planet.

It is widely claimed that crisps (or potato chips) were invented by chef George Crum in 1853 at his Saratoga Springs restaurant, Moon's Lake House. Steamship owner Cornelius Vanderbilt allegedly sent a meal back to the kitchen because the french fries were too thick and pale. In protest, Crum sliced the potatoes paper thin and fried them to a crisp. Vanderbilt loved them, and the 'Saratoga chips' became legendary.

It's a good story. Only it seems to be false.

The earliest known recipe for crisps, or potato chips, is in English optician William Kitchener's cookbook, The Cook's Oracle, published in 1817 – 36 years before Crum – but it's entirely probable that people had been frying thinly sliced potatoes for long before that.

If you enjoy eating crisps while sitting in the comfort of your own home, it is hard to describe how mind-blowing they taste after you've been running for several hours. The sensation of the salty crisps on your tongue is out of this world. And you also get the added smugness, knowing you've burned far more calories than you'll be consuming.

Running a self-supported marathon was a unique experience. There was no fanfare, no crowds, no mile markers, route directions or feed stations. We had no expectation of a finish time, but it also made it tough to summon the motivation to continue.

The final five miles were some of the toughest of any marathon I have taken part in. My legs had nothing left and it became increasingly difficult to justify continuing. I had eaten two bags of crisps, three-quarters of a round of cheese sandwiches, and now it was time to bring out the pork pie. I stuffed the final quarter of the cheese sandwich into my mouth as I unwrapped it.

'Oh god. What iz zeez?' said Daniel.

'It's a pwork pwie,' I said, mid-mouthful.

'A what?'

'He said it's a pork pie,' snapped Charles.

'A pork pie? What iz zeez pork pie?'

'It's pwork mweat cwovered in pwastry.'

'Iz it like zeez other zings you eat. Sausage rolled?'

'Swausage woll?' I said, swallowing the rest of the sandwich. 'No, pork pies are very different. The pork is hard, and the pastry is hard, not crispy.'

'And you eat zeez cold?'

'Yes, always cold. I carried a big one for the whole of that ultramarathon we did with you, but I didn't eat it. Do you want to try some?'

'Er... ok,' said Marta.

I unwrapped the clingfilm and held out the pork pie, which I had already cut into pieces and spread with English mustard. Daniel and Marta both took a piece.

'Charles? Pork pie?'

He had been very quiet for the last few miles, which was a tell-tale sign he too was struggling. He was usually full of confidence and setting the pace, but occasionally we would see he was human, and he would express his pain and suffering through silence. He gave a brief shake of his head but didn't even look up.

Having lived in Barcelona all of their lives and being used to the fine array of Spanish foods on offer, I was intrigued to hear Daniel and Marta's verdict on the humble pork pie. The often underrated, but second greatest achievement of British cuisine – behind the potato chip.

As we walked up yet another hill, they both chewed slowly on their piece of pork pie.

'Well, what do you think?'

Daniel and Marta smiled at each other and nodded slowly as they finished chewing.

'Err...' said Marta.

'It izz... er... it izz different,' said Daniel.

'Is different good?'

'Different izz... er... different.'

I took a piece and put it into my mouth. The pork pie had been slowly sweating in my rucksack all day and the meat was slimy and warm and the pastry soft and slightly damp. It tasted revolting.

'No... wait... this is... it's not supposed to taste like that.'

'Oh, good,' they both said, spitting their mouthfuls into the grass.

I obviously ate the rest of it, though.

I gave them a proper pork pie a few days later, and they really enjoyed it. Or at least they made a convincing job of pretending to.

We had worked out a rough route in our heads beforehand, hoping it would make up a full marathon distance, but as we neared the school where we had started that morning, it became clear we were going to be about a mile short.

'I think we will have to continue past the school for half a mile and then run back to make it up to the full distance,' I said, assuming the others would agree with me.

'Yes, abzolutely,' said Marta.

'Fuck that,' said Charles. 'I'm done. I'm stopping here.'

'But you won't have done a full marathon?'

'Who cares? I just wanted to do a long run, and 25 hilly miles is plenty long enough for me, thanks.'

'Go on, Charles. You can't stop now. You izz so close,' said Daniel.

'Nope. You go on. I'm done.'

'Charles, seriously, stop being such a loser,' I said. 'You can't DNF when you're so close to the end.'

'DNF? What are you talking about? How can I DNF something that isn't even a real thing?'

'Because we set out to run a marathon and if you only run 25 miles, then I'm putting you down as Did Not Finish.'

'Putting me down where?' he laughed. 'Who is going to care about how far we ran?'

'I care,' I said. 'I'll always think of you as a quitter.'

Daniel and Marta both laughed.

'Let's leave him here,' said Daniel. 'I didn't think he would be able to complete it anyway.'

This predictably got Charles riled.

'Of course I could complete it if I wanted to. I just don't want to.'

'We don't think you av got what it takes,' said Marta.

'Fine, you bastards, I'll run the final mile with you. Not because I have to, just to shut you up.'

Our watches were all showing slightly different distances, and each of us stopped running the second our own ticked over to 26.2 miles. The four of us were spread out over a few hundred metres, not wanting to run a step further than absolutely necessary. Charles's watch was more conservative than the rest of ours, so we made him keep running up and down the road for a few minutes after we had all finished. We still had an hour until the end of the school day, so retired to the local pub for a quick burger and beer.

It was a fantastic day and proved a different kind of challenge. Without that incentive of a medal, a goody bag, the motivation of the crowd to cheer us on, or the looming prospect of receiving a DNF on the results page, there was nothing enticing us to continue, other than our own willpower. And while Charles had shown complete apathy towards the end, he seemed glad that we had persuaded him to complete the last mile. Any suggestion that he was a quitter was eradicated a few months later when he completed a 100-mile run.

To make the day even more special, the children came out of school with medals they had made for all of us. Well, I say medals, they were bits of paper with 'wel don' written on them, tied to a ribbon, but they felt like the best medals I'd ever received. I'm not sure Charles felt the same.

SEVEN

Despite my good intentions, my training for the Dart 10k swim had not gone to plan. A friend of mine, Matt, signed up too, and while he trained in the pool several times a week, and combined it with regular long open-water swims, I did almost nothing. Our plan had been to train together, but I slipped so far behind him in both speed and technique that I felt like I would only be holding him back.

The Dart 10k follows the river downstream, and I sort of naively hoped that I could leisurely float down with the current. What I had neglected to consider is that it's a tidal estuary, and the race starts at high water. It is not until you are well into the swim that you begin to notice any benefit from the tide or current. And even with a bit of assistance, 6.2 miles is still a bloody long way to swim. Leisurely floating down the river was definitely not an option.

Matt and I did go out for one open water swim together. We met at the beach and the sea was far rougher than we had anticipated. But as we had committed to it, we headed out and swam for about 45 minutes. I found the rolling of the waves really disorientating and spent half the time trying to work out where Matt had gone, and the other half of the time trying to stop myself from being sick. There would be no big rolling waves to contend with in the Dart, but it wasn't so much the waves that were the problem. It was the fear and panic that I felt when swimming in open water.

This was partly the fear of what lurked beneath. But I knew that was mostly in my head, and that was secondary to the fear of just not being confident at swimming for any length of time. I knew I should be able to swim for a long distance in the sea, because I had done it before, but being out there with Matt pulling further ahead with every stroke, it felt like I was a beginner once again, all the way back in Stroke Development 4. I foolishly declined Matt's further offers to swim together again and tried to push thoughts of the Dart 10k to the back of my mind.

The chaos of family life provided a welcome distraction from thinking about the Dart 10k. We moved to Devon in the summer of 2013, having sold our house in Northampton and found a lovely place to rent on a farm. We thought we would maybe live there a year or two, to give us time to find a house to buy. At the time of writing this – seven and half years later – we are still here. It has been a wonderful place to live. Despite being in the middle of nowhere, living on a busy working farm means there are always things going on. The house we live in was once part of the farm's stable block, and the remaining stables and barns in the yard are still used at various stages of the year for horses, cows and sheep.

During lambing season, all the ewes pregnant with multiple lambs are kept in an enclosure just outside our house until they have given birth, at which point they are taken back out into the fields. Any orphaned lambs, or lambs rejected by their mothers, are bottle-fed for several weeks until they too can go out into the fields. Each spring, Layla, Leo and Kitty get to help out with the bottle-feeding before and after school.

As well as all the farm animals, there have been many dogs – both working and pets – and several cats on the farm, too. In my book *Life's a Beach*, I wrote about two kittens – Fred and Rocky – who came to the farm soon after we moved in. During the cold winter months, Fred would often emerge from underneath our car after short car journeys. He had been climbing into the car engine to keep warm. Either that or he was an adrenaline junky. For almost a year afterwards, we had to conduct a full sweep of the underside of the car before driving anywhere to check for any stowaways. He eventually got too big to fit in the engine. The reason he got so big was because he was pregnant. It turned out he was a she. And so was his sister Rocky. Within a few weeks, the farm cats Fred and Rocky each gave birth to a large litter of kittens.

One afternoon, I was in the kitchen and caught a glimpse of Rocky coming in through the cat-flap with something in her mouth as she crossed the room and disappeared up the stairs. She had a habit of sneaking into our house to enjoy the warmth, but as she appeared to be carrying something, I thought I better go and investigate, rather than have to clear up the remains of some half-eaten animal later in the day. When I went upstairs, I found Rocky in one of the bedrooms, emerging from underneath the duvet on Kitty's bed. I lifted it up and discovered she had brought all five of her kittens inside and made a warm nest for them in the bedding. Thankfully, the children were all at school, otherwise we would have likely ended up keeping all of them. We settled on one. A female mackerel tabby. We named her Moomin.

We had two cats when we lived in Northampton: Father Dougal and Batfink (Finky). When we moved to Devon, we left Father Dougal with our neighbour Doug, because Doug and his wife Christine became very attached to Father Dougal (or Basil, as they renamed him), and he spent more time with them next door than at our house. Finky had adapted to life on the farm in Devon really well. She was already ten when we moved, and was enjoying a chilled-out retirement, so despite all the potential adventures and exploration opportunities on the farm, rarely strayed beyond our garden wall. But she seemed to welcome the company of a new cat and tolerated Moomin's occasionally irritating kitten habits.

Living on a farm had not been part of the grand plan when we decided to move to Devon; it just happened to be the only house we could find to rent. But it unexpectedly turned out to be one of the best things that could have happened to us, and a magnificent environment for the children to grow up in.

'Your children will grow up so quickly,' people always tell us. 'Make sure you enjoy them when they are young.'

Rachel and I don't want to wish away the years, but we were also getting a little bored with our family outings consisting solely of visits to play parks, petting zoos and soft play centres. We were looking forward to a time when we could start having more exciting adventures as a family. And by adventures, I mean walks of more than half a mile, or a bike ride that didn't end with me wheeling at least two bikes and often carrying (dragging) a screaming child too. Things seemed to be improving, as over time our 'adventures' slowly increased in length and duration.

During this year's school holidays, Rachel and I decided we would try to keep our visits to play parks, petting zoos and soft play centres to a minimum, and become a bit more adventurous as a family.

I was a fairly fit and active child. I spent more than my fair share of time playing computer games and watching TV, but I also spent a lot of time outside – building dens, playing football or riding my bike.

My parents weren't pushy with me or my sister when it came to sport. I liked playing lots of sports but was distinctly average at everything I tried. This worked out well for everyone as it kept me active, getting involved in lots of different sports and activities, but I did not show enough promise in any particular sport to warrant devoting an unnecessary amount of time or money to it.

When I was growing up, we went on an annual holiday to the Lake District with a couple of other families with similar aged children to my sister and me. Each day, the parents would get us all to walk up a peak or two and we moaned incessantly about being made to climb mountains. But every walk ended up being so much more fun than we expected. We stopped for a picnic lunch, made up games, told stories, and jumped in as many tarns, rivers and bogs as we could find, and were always glad we had done it by the time we made it home.

I would like our children to be fit and active too, and I also want to avoid being a pushy parent. So rather than signing them up to lots of different sports clubs and activities against their will, Rachel and I decided we would continue to encourage (force) them on family activities. We also hope that they will see the satisfaction and sense of achievement felt by Rachel and me when we complete our own events, and for them to perhaps feel inspired and want to get involved.

On the last day of the school summer term, we picked up the children from school and headed to Dorset for four days' camping with some old school friends from Northampton, including Mark who I travelled across America with in *Not Tonight, Josephine*, and completed the ultramarathon with in *Chasing Trails* earlier that year.

We had a wonderful few days exploring the Jurassic Coast, fossil hunting and taking advantage of the spacious camping field, with its toilet block that felt like a half-day walk away.

While my fitness seemed to have stagnated since the ultramarathon in February, Mark's had skyrocketed. He persuaded me to join him for a run early on the first morning and we set off along the South West Coast Path towards West Bay. I had hoped that the hills of South Devon would have given me an advantage over Mark on Dorset's hills, but, despite Mark living in the relative plains of Kent, he skipped up the steep slopes effortlessly and I was left eating his dust.

Our campsite was at the foot of Golden Cap, near the village of Seatown. Golden Cap is the highest peak along the south coast of Great Britain, and it dominates the surrounding coastline. It was far too high for those Romans, and it is extremely unlikely they ever dared venture onto its slopes.

It was impossible to escape the lure of Golden Cap sitting high above our campsite. So on the second morning, I declined Mark's offer of a longer run, and headed up Golden Cap solo. When I reached the top (I walked almost the entire way, but I was wearing my running kit, so let's call it a run), the low-lying cloud reduced the visibility to only a few metres and I couldn't even see the path I had followed up. Missing out on the views that were so tantalisingly there yet not there just made me adamant that I would have to climb it again.

'Can I walk up it with you?' said Layla, during breakfast when I told them about my 'run'.

'Of course you can. When do you want to go? Shall we go today?'

'Ok. Is it hard?'

'It is quite hard, but you'll be able to get to the top, no problem.'

Climbing Golden Cap became Layla's own mini adventure. She packed herself a backpack with some water and snacks, and somehow convinced me into buying her sweets from the campsite shop to give her energy while walking. I suggested to Rachel that we make it a family trip and encourage Leo and Kitty along too, but Layla wanted this to be her thing and didn't want her younger brother and sister to get in on the act. Mostly, she didn't want them to have sweets, too.

Later that morning, we made it to the top of Golden Cap, while Rachel built an impressive sandcastle with Leo and Kitty on the beach below. She found it tough (Layla, not Rachel), but felt a tremendous sense of achievement on reaching the top, and I felt a deep sense of pride that she had instigated it herself.

EIGHT

A few weeks later, we took the ferry to France for a fortnight's camping holiday. We strapped three bikes to the back of our small hatchback and fixed another on the roof next to a roof box stuffed full of camping equipment. I drew the short straw and there was no room for my bike.

Layla and Leo have both fully embraced cycling. Part of the reason is because they both learned to ride their bikes while we still lived in Northampton. We were a few minutes' walk from an extensive park with miles of flat, paved paths. They both learned on the same wooden balance bike and progressed to pedal bikes soon after their third birthdays. We had moved to Devon just before Kitty turned two, and options for Kitty to learn to cycle were very limited.

We made after-hours visits to some local tennis courts, and Kitty learned to ride her bike by doing laps of the courts. She got the hang of it pretty quickly but going round and round the same patch of concrete repeatedly soon became boring for her. So, we tried taking our bikes in the car to a proper cycle path, but this backfired when Kitty realised her brother and sister were much faster than her and no matter how fast she pedalled she couldn't keep up with them. From that point on, Kitty's relationship with bicycles was doomed. As far as she was concerned, bikes were evil.

But maybe if we were in France, on holiday, things would be different? Kitty was a week away from turning five and had said she didn't want us to bring her stupid bike on holiday. We had obviously ignored her in the hope she would grow to love it.

Our first campsite in the Vendee on the west coast of France was small enough that the children could cycle around safely on their own. A year previously, at the campsite where we stayed during my Ironman, Layla and Leo experienced the independence of being able to explore the campsite on their bikes together, with Kitty often trotting along behind on foot. Now that Kitty was older and very capable of riding her bike, she was able to join her brother and sister on their cycling explorations.

After about 10 minutes they returned, claiming they had explored every inch of the campsite and there was nothing else to see.

'We cycled absolutely miles,' said Leo. 'How long have we been gone for?'

'About 10 minutes,' I said.

'Is that all? How far do you think we cycled?'

'Absolutely miles.'

'Seriously. How far do you think we cycled?'

'I don't know. Maybe a mile?'

'A mile! I bet we did much more than that. I reckon we

did 50 miles. Can I borrow your GPS watch?'

'Er, yes, I suppose so. Don't break it.'

'That's not fair. What about me? Mummy, can I borrow yours?' said Layla, deftly unstrapping the watch from Rachel's arm like a magician.

'Sure,' said Rachel, who had her head buried in a book and didn't even seem to notice.

'That's not fair!' said Kitty, getting off her bike and sinking into a camping chair.

'You can share the watches,' I said. 'Take it in turns.'

'No. I hate cycling anyway,' said Kitty.

Layla and Leo spent the next half an hour doing laps of the campsite, which should have been relaxing for Rachel and me had we not had Kitty moaning next to us. Layla and Leo returned every couple of minutes asking, 'guess how far we've cycled?' But it was fun to at least see the two of them getting enjoyment out of exercise and challenging themselves a little. Hopefully, it would soon rub off on Kitty.

The following morning, Rachel and I tried going for a run with the three children alongside on their bikes. It didn't prove very successful. We were running too slowly to keep Layla and Leo satisfied, and Kitty insisted on stopping every 10 metres to remove an item of clothing or to have a sip from her drinking bottle. With all unnecessary items of clothing removed, and her drinking bottle empty, she then stopped every 10 metres to put various items of clothing back on, or to fix her imaginary bike issues such as her reflectors being too dirty and her bike bell not being quite pingy enough.

At one point, I stopped to try to convince Kitty that her wheels were perfectly round – despite her insistence that they weren't – and I looked up and discovered Rachel, Leo and Layla had disappeared off into the distance without us. This made Kitty even more irrational, and she threw her bike down on the floor in a strop. I told her if she didn't ride her bike she would have to run. She said that was fine with her and ran off up the path to catch up with the others. I was left standing alone with a four-year-old's bike with its wheels not quite round enough, dirty reflectors and a disappointingly un-pingy bell.

I climbed aboard. By the time I reached the others, my knees were bruised all over from catching them on the handlebars.

'This is fun,' said Rachel, who had jogged alongside Layla and Leo for a further mile up the coast, before returning to meet up with me and Kitty. 'We should do it more often.'

'Fun? You try negotiating with Kitty next time,' I said.

'Well, you obviously didn't do a very good job negotiating. You're riding her bike.'

'I didn't choose to ride her bike! I would much rather be running than squashed onto this stupid bike,' I said.

'See!' said Kitty. 'Even Daddy agrees that it's a stupid bike.'

'No, I didn't mean that. I meant it's a stupid bike for a grown man to be riding. It's a perfectly decent bike for you to be riding.'

'It's not. It's stupid. I hate it.'

We didn't go on any more family bike rides that holiday, and Kitty's stupid bike stayed lying on the floor by the tent.

On one of the mornings, we managed to book all three children into the campsite's Kids Club. They were reluctant, but agreed to give it a try, on the condition it didn't have to be forever. It was flattering that they would rather spend time with their parents than a group of other children, but also bloody annoying.

After checking them in and realising they were the only kids who weren't French, Rachel and I headed off guiltily and chose to spend our 'free time' going for a run together up the coast. Heading north towards the town of Saint-Jean-de-Monts, we made decent progress, taking advantage of the flat terrain and the fact that the clouds had made their first appearance of the week. The dry and dusty landscape of the Vendee made a pleasant change from the hills of South Devon. There are long stretches of land between the towns on this stretch of coast with no development. But during the summer months, when tourists flock to the region from all over, these patches of barren land become locations for seasonal entertainment. It was a surreal experience to run past a small traditional French boulangerie with the wasteland next door occupied by a big top for a travelling circus. We then passed a quaint little French chapel, which had been there for hundreds of years, now sitting in the shadow of the grandstand for a monster truck show. Is that what Jesus would have wanted?

The gaps between houses grew smaller and smaller as we reached the edge of Saint-Jean-de-Monts.

'How far do you want to go?' I asked Rachel. 'We've done five miles already.'

'Shall we do another mile and then turn back? 12 miles seems like a good distance to do. We might as well make the most of this flat ground. It's amazing.'

'Sounds good to me.'

We ran along the town's impressive waterfront, with high-rise apartment buildings and dozens of bars and restaurants. At the far end of town, we reached the six-mile point and turned to begin the homeward journey. It was at this point we realised there had been an almighty tailwind the entire way, which was why we had been effortlessly flying up the coast.

It took us considerably longer to run back to the campsite. And through it all, Rachel was in a horrendous mood. She became extremely quiet and ignored all of my attempts at conversation, as though the wind was somehow my fault.

'THE WIND MAKES ME SO ANGRY!' she shouted.

'So I can see,' I shouted back. 'Why do you hate it so much?'

'It drives me mad. It makes running so much harder and it makes a really annoying noise in my ears.'

'Ha, an annoying noise? It's just wind!'

'YOU ARE AN ANNOYING NOISE IN MY EARS, TOO.'

'That's a bit harsh! Why are you so cross with me?'

'Because you're acting like the wind is absolutely fine.'

'Well, there's not much we can do about it. It's not going to go away just because you get angry with it. And it's definitely not my fault.'

'Can you please just BE QUIET? I'm not in the mood.'

We made it back to the campsite with a few minutes to spare before lunchtime at the Kids Club. Rachel calmed down as soon as we stopped running. We went to meet the children, hoping they would have had such a great time that they would want to go back after lunch, and then for the rest of the week. As we waited outside, Layla was sitting near the window doing a drawing. She saw us approach and then scribbled something onto a piece of paper and held it up to the glass.

'*THIS IS TORTURE,*' it said, and she gave us a sarcastic smile.

Rachel and I both laughed, and then looked up to see the Kids Club organiser walk over to Layla and ask her what she had showed us. Layla tried to hide it, but the lady picked up the piece of paper and read the words. During our very brief conversation with the organiser that morning, we established her English was very, very good. She gave a little laugh and then smiled at us through the window. We gave our apologies, but Layla never showed her face at Kids Club again.

Leo and Kitty's morning fared a little better, but not well enough for them to want to go again.

'Looks like it's Daddy Day Care at the pool for the rest of the week,' said Rachel.

'What do you mean? What about you?'

'No, the pool is too cold for me. You're much better at the water slides than me.'

'Better at the water slides? What does that even mean?'

'I don't know. I'm just really enjoying my book at the moment.'

'Are you still angry with me because it was windy on our run?'

'Maybe a little.'

The water slide had been Leo's nemesis all week. He had been desperate to try it, but each time we climbed to the top together, he changed his mind and we had to do the walk of shame back down the crowded steps. Eventually, on our last full day at the campsite, he went up on his own and took the plunge. He enjoyed it so much that he went on it another 48 times that day.

Due to a last-minute change of plan when booking the holiday, and a bad knowledge of French geography (both of which Rachel blamed on me), we discovered that what we thought was going to be a two-hour drive to the second campsite was actually going to be six. By the time we had taken down the tent and packed the car, it was midday, and the sun was out in full force. The six-hour journey turned into eight, in a heavily laden car with no air conditioning. Rachel sat in the passenger seat fanning herself with a magazine like a diva. Layla and Kitty moaned constantly about the heat in the back, but Leo was ominously quiet. We stopped for a McDonald's halfway there, where Leo revealed the reason for his silence by projectile vomiting all over the floor. Fortunately, we were at a quiet outside table, so it wasn't too much of a spectacle.

We made it to our campsite on the banks of the Dordogne just after 8pm. The campsite was well worth the extra drive, and I was instantly forgiven for the administrative error. Rachel took the kids to the pool for a swim while I put up the tent. It is nice when children offer to help, but for certain jobs – particularly putting up tents – it takes twice as long if they get involved.

I cracked open a warm beer that had been incubating in the car boot and rolled out the groundsheet. By the time I pegged it down, I was onto my second beer. Rachel returned soon after 9pm, as I was just finishing my fourth. The tent was up, in a slightly wonky way, but neither of us cared.

Part of the reason we had chosen this campsite was for its proximity to the Dordogne river. The campsite had direct access to a small sandy beach where the river was perfect for swimming. I had ambitious plans to treat this week as a last-minute training camp to prepare for the Dart 10K, which was still looming over me, and a little over a week away.

The closer it got to the event, the more nervous I became, and I was forced to admit to myself that I was completely unprepared. My previous longest swim – as part of the Ironman – had been 2.4 miles. And that was almost a year earlier. Since then, I had not once swum further than a mile. *How would I be able to swim ten kilometres? SIX POINT TWO MILES?* It sounded more and more ridiculous each time I thought about it.

In the Vendee, I had been intimidated by the almighty Atlantic Ocean, and a stretch of coastline I was unfamiliar with. I went into the sea almost every day, but only to play in the waves with the children. My wetsuit and goggles remained in the car. But all was not yet lost. I still had a week in the Dordogne to build up my confidence and prepare myself for the Dart.

On our first morning at the new site, full of good intentions, and full of croissants and pain au chocolat, I took my goggles down to the river. The kids had been reluctant to swim in the river, claiming the swimming pool was WAY BETTER, but they soon realised the pleasure in drifting with the current, and the peculiar enjoyment of the earthy taste of the river water on your lips.

A little upstream from the campsite's beach, the river

widened and became only a few inches deep, which would make swimming upstream a little problematic, as I was yet to perfect my salmon technique. Just downstream from the campsite beach it did the same, leaving only a relatively small section where it was deep enough to swim. This was great for peace of mind, knowing the children could not be swept away anywhere, but not so great for endurance swim training.

I did spend about ten minutes that first morning swimming against the current in my own never-ending pool, but it was incredibly boring, and a little disconcerting having a beach full of holidaymakers watching me fruitlessly battling the river. In that moment, my Dart 10k training schedule was dramatically re-written. I would now rely on winging it.

Exercise was not completely neglected during the week, though. To try to offset some of the vast amounts of food and drink consumed, Rachel and I each went out for a few short runs. I usually went first thing in the morning, as Rachel falls into a deep coma when she's in a tent and is very reluctant to get out of her sleeping bag. After it had cooled down in the evening, Rachel would go off on her run, conveniently just when it was time to cook the dinner. I definitely got the bum deal.

I took my bike out a couple of times too, but only for very short loops of the surrounding countryside. It was too hot for any long rides, and this week was all about splashing around in the pool and river.

Kitty celebrated her fifth birthday during the week, so we booked a canoe trip down the Dordogne. We were driven up the river in a minibus with a few other families, towing a trailer stacked with canoes. They assigned us two boats between the five of us, gave us paddles, buoyancy aids and a very quick briefing (*'s'il vous plaît ne vous noyez pas'* – *please don't drown*), and then told us we were on our own. All we had to do was paddle downriver back to the campsite at our own speed.

This stretch of the Dordogne is stunning, with imposing cliffs on each bank, and a spectacular chateau revealing itself around every sweeping bend. The most impressive was Château de Montfort, which sits perilously on a rocky outcrop on the clifftop. A large section of the castle is built on an overhanging rock, like the sort of place the baddie would live in a Disney movie. These castles were built in such ludicrous locations partly as a defence – nobody other than the bravest of climbers could attack the castle from the riverside – but also as a statement for all who saw it. And what a statement it was. Château de Montfort was named after Simon de Monfort, who celebrated having a castle named after him by burning it to the ground in 1214. It was rebuilt and then destroyed three more times in the following centuries. Imagine the insurance premium.

We stopped for a picnic on the other side of the river, close enough to view Chateau de Monfort, but far enough away in case this was the day the castle suddenly realised it had been defying gravity all these years. We had brought a simple but delicious lunch of baguettes, cheese and tomatoes, which we stored in the canoe's watertight barrels, and a couple of lukewarm French lagers to wash it down.

We all had a swim in the shallows after lunch and waved as a couple of familiar faces from the minibus passed us, and we then climbed into our canoes and continued down the Dordogne. We stopped again for a few more swims and played on a rope swing attached to a tree overhanging the river.

Layla, Leo and Kitty were having a brilliant time, but not as much as Rachel and me who decided there and then that floating down the river in a canoe is the greatest way to travel.

It took us almost two hours to cover the three miles, and I tried not to think about the fact I would soon have to swim over twice that distance, without the help of the fast-flowing river. And without the aid of a canoe.

A couple of days later, we booked ourselves onto another – much longer – canoe trip. This one departed from our campsite with our destination over nine miles downstream. We had brought with us more food for this trip and stopped regularly at nice swimming spots to eat and swim. The Dordogne valley continued to amaze us. It was faster flowing than our previous trip, which required a little more effort to guide the canoe down the gentle rapids, avoiding rocks and the shallows. We kept a mental note of little waterside restaurants we might come back to later that day (but never did) and rated other campsites as we passed (none were as good as ours). Along the calmer sections, we all took it in turns to float down the river behind the canoe. While lying in the water on my back, looking up at one of the many chateaus dotting the riverbank, I remembered it was a year to the day since I completed my Ironman. I felt like a different person to the man I was before that day. Today's triathlon consisted of eating, floating and canoeing, and it is a combination I would highly recommend.

Nearly four hours later, we arrived at the designated collection point, dragged our canoes up onto the sand, bought an ice-cream from a kiosk and waited for the minibus to come pick us up.

The following day we would begin the long journey home, and in two days I would take part in the Dart 10k swim. My planned intensive French swim training camp hadn't worked out as planned. But I looked around at the smiling, sun-blushed, ice-cream smeared faces of my family, and had no regrets whatsoever.

NINE

We arrived home from France the day before the Dart 10k. During our holiday, I had tried to avoid thinking about the swim. Because each time I did and realised the ridiculousness of what I had signed up to, an intense feeling of unease and nausea swept over me. But I never once thought about pulling out. I was committed. And as daunting as it felt, I was still willing to at least give it a go.

My friend – and fellow first timer – Matt had prepared well. He swam regularly in the sea throughout the summer, and despite getting nastily stung by a jellyfish on the nose a few days before, was considerably more excited about the event than I was. Matt's encounter with the jellyfish had given me yet another thing to feel anxious about.

I too had spent a lot of time in the water over the summer, but I was either in a canoe, on a bodyboard, or whizzing down a water slide. None of which are ideal preparation for a 10k swim.

I shared a lift to the start with Matt and his friend Charlie. Charlie was down from Bristol for the weekend and is a seasoned pro at endurance sport, having competed in Ironmans, ultra-marathons and some unimaginably long bike rides. He recently cycled from Bristol to London and back... in one go. A distance of 600 kilometres.

We parked on a side street in Totnes and walked the half mile to the start at Steamers Quay on the banks of the River Dart. We arrived early, but swimmers were already standing around in small groups ready to go, their wetsuits pulled up as far as their waists. The lack of wind after the recent storms, the soft early morning light, and the mist still clinging to the surface of the water, made for a calm and almost ethereal atmosphere.

Looking around at the other swimmers, I was reminded of one of the pleasing benefits of open water swimming events, which I had also noticed when I took part in the Plymouth Breakwater Swim the previous year: the complete lack of intimidation brought on by the appearance of athleticism amongst other competitors. At the start of a running or cycling race, you look around at the men and women who surround you, and everyone always looks fitter, stronger and younger. This is not the case with swimming. Swimmers come in all shapes, sizes and ages. It is absolutely impossible to guess how good someone is at swimming by looking at them on dry land. Unless they happen to have gills. If you are at the start line of a 5k run and standing alongside a hugely overweight 80-year-old, providing you've done a bit of training, you would probably fancy your chances against them over the distance. But, when it comes to swimming, there is every chance you'll be eating their wake within the first few metres.

Also, cyclists, and to some extent runners, can make a show (or more often than not, a pretence) of their ability with fancy equipment and attire – expensive trainers or a top of the range bike. But all wetsuits are pretty much identical. Put on a black wetsuit, a pair of goggles and a swim hat, and an experienced swimmer looks virtually indistinguishable from a beginner.

The Outdoor Swimming Society – the organisation behind the Dart 10k – was founded by wild swimmer Kate Rew in 2006. The OSS promotes, encourages and advises on outdoor swimming in the UK and abroad, and the Dart 10k was the first of the three swimming events it now organises – the other two being the Bantham Swoosh in South Devon and the Hurly Burly in the Mawddach estuary in North Wales. 800 swimmers had taken part in the Dart 10k on the Saturday, and another 800 were taking part today.

Despite the large numbers of swimmers assembling for the event, it felt remarkably understated and relaxed. But there was still a palpable sense of nervousness in the air.

Registration took place in a small marquee where we collected our swim hat, and marshals held out tubs of Vaseline for swimmers to apply to their chafing areas.

All dignity goes out the window at swimming events. Men and women stand around in front of each other in various stages of undress, while liberally applying dollops of lubricant to their genitals mid-conversation.

Swimmers for the Dart 10k were split into waves, depending on our expected finishing times. Each wave was given a different coloured swim hat. Unlike running events, the slower swimmers were to start first, otherwise they ran the risk of running out of water as the tide went out and would be left stranded on the mud. This idea secretly appealed to me, as I much preferred the idea of a 10k walk to a 10k swim.

The ghostly silence was broken by the booming voice of OSS chief announcer Paul Smith, whose energy, enthusiasm and obscenely loud voice demonstrated that this was a job he was born to do. He warned us we had ten minutes until our swim start.

Matt, Charlie and I posed for a couple of 'before' photos, and I forced a smile to try to convince myself I was excited. And then it was time for our wave to assemble for our briefing. We huddled together in the starting pen and Paul Smith said a few words about safety – *stick to the part of the river that the support crew direct you to and if you get into difficulty roll onto your back and wave your arms in the air.* There was a brief description of the route too, although the benefit of swimming down a river is there is not too much danger of getting lost.

This was it.

6.2 miles of water lay between us and the finish. This

would be well over two-and-a-half times further than I had ever swum before, and I felt overwhelmed by the enormity of the challenge I had set myself. I remembered how weak my arms had felt after the Ironman swim over a year earlier. And since then, I had done almost nothing to prepare myself for this gigantic step up. Oh well, it was too late to worry about it now. It was my own stupid fault. It was time to get it over with.

The klaxon sounded, and swimmers entered the water. The OSS had made it clear it wasn't a race. As we waded down the ramp into the river, I spat into my goggles, gave them a final rinse and pulled them on over my head. I wished Matt and Charlie good luck, took the final few steps down the slippery slipway, until the slippery slipway slipped away, and I was swimming.

After the initial shock of the cold water creeping down the back of my wetsuit had passed, the water temperature was quite pleasant, and I took a few strokes of breaststroke out towards the riverbank on the opposite side which we would stick to for the first few hundred metres.

The water at the Totnes end of the Dart is brackish, meaning it is a combination of the tidal seawater and the freshwater from the river. The salinity of the water would increase the closer we got to the finish. This section of river is fairly narrow. I had soon reached the opposite bank and, as everyone around me was now swimming front crawl, I put my head down and began making strokes.

After just 200m, I knew the swim was going to be much

tougher than I expected. My shoulders felt tired and heavy already, and each stroke felt like a considerable effort. I was woefully out-of-my-depth. But only metaphorically. The Dart is quite shallow in places, especially as we were hugging the shoreline so closely. This made the temptation to stand up overwhelming and on a couple of occasions during that first half mile, I plunged my feet into the gloopy riverbed and stood up, adjusting my goggles to justify the brief timeout, when I was actually standing up because I just didn't want to swim. A nearby safety kayaker asked if I was alright.

I was not alright.

I was not ready for this and angry with myself for being so cavalier about my preparation. I should just admit that I was an idiot for signing up to this event and pull out before it got a lot worse.

But how much of what I was feeling was because of the swim? I had covered less than half a mile. I knew I should be able to swim half a mile without feeling this terrible. What I was feeling was fear. And fear was something I should be able to overcome.

'Are you ok?' the kayaker said again. I had just been standing there, deep in thought, and had not noticed she had paddled closer.

'Yes, sorry,' I said. 'I was just taking a little moment to… err… sort out my goggles. They are all sorted now. Thanks.'

I pulled them on and took a deep breath. That muddy riverbed would be there again on occasions if I needed it.

But I couldn't walk the entire 10k swim. I had signed up for this stupid event, so I was going to damn well at least try to get through it. I didn't know if I could, but I was not going to pull out in the first few hundred metres simply because I felt a bit scared. If I was going to be marked down as DNF, then I wanted it to come after I had swum further than half a mile. I dipped my head back into the murky water and counted out 50 strokes of front crawl.

We passed the distinctive Cormorant Tree – a dead tree overhanging the river that is so named because it is a popular nesting spot for herons. Only joking, it's a popular spot for egrets. The splashing of 800 swimmers must have looked a strange sight to the lone curious cormorant perched on one of its branches.

It had been raining continuously for 24 hours prior to the swim, which meant that the water was perhaps murkier than usual because of all the surface runoff. The water quality of the Dart is rated highly, but because of the silt, sediment, runoff from the fields, and the fact that 800 swimmers were kicking it all up, there was no visibility whatsoever under the water. My expectations of having a three-hour underwater wildlife tour were dashed. The terrible weather had also resulted in a lot of branches making their way into the river, providing some additional floating obstacles for us.

The banks of the river near to Totnes are supported by walls built by inmates from Dartmoor prison. As the tidal estuary has to contend with some high winds and big tides, these walls have taken a fair beating over the years. A section – known as the 'hole in the wall' – has disappeared completely, and the river has flooded the neighbouring land, creating its own little marsh and ecosystem. A kayaker stood guard to keep us in the main part of the river and prevent us from slipping into this other world.

About a third of the way into the swim, the river starts a series of long sweeping bends. When you look at these twists and turns on a map, you imagine that you are going to be whooshed around these bends like you're in a lazy river at a water park. In reality, each of these bends is over a mile long and there is no whooshing whatsoever.

We could see the impressive sight of Sharpham House up on the hillside to our right. This Georgian manor house is now home to a successful wine and cheese making business.

I had paddled this section of the Dart in a kayak before. As a present for my dad's 60th birthday, my sister and I booked kayaks for the three of us for a half-day excursion. We set off from Totnes with the aim to meet my mum, Rachel and Layla (aged two) first at Sharpham and then at a pub in the village of Tuckenhay for a late lunch. Rachel was heavily pregnant with Leo at the time so opted not to kayak.

We had a brilliant morning, and it didn't take us long to reach the first stop at Sharpham, where we moored our kayaks at the boathouse and walked up the path to the main building. We met my mum, Rachel and Layla and enjoyed a fun wine and cheese tasting session, before retracing our steps – a little tipsily – back to our kayaks.

We continued at a leisurely pace towards our destination for lunch in the village of Tuckenhay at the head of Bow Creek. Our paddling had been assisted by the current and we were protected from the wind by the high banks of the river. As soon as we turned right into Bow Creek, the wind hit us full in the face, blowing us back out into the main river. Combined with the increasing pull of the current – which we were now fighting against – we paddled as hard as we could and crept forward at a sea snail's pace. But the moment we paused to rest, the wind and current pushed us back in the direction we had come. I don't think the cheese and wine had helped our efforts.

We had no option but to climb into the water and wade up the creek, pulling our kayaks behind us. The water was just above knee depth, but the riverbed was a thick squelchy clay, and extremely difficult to walk through. It was utterly exhausting, but we laughed at the absurdity of how our little kayak adventure had panned out.

Sitting in the pub garden waiting for us, my mum, Rachel and Layla caught sight of three pathetic looking specimens making their final trudge to the end of the creek.

'I thought you were supposed to sit in those things?' called Rachel as we neared.

'You should try paddling against the current into this wind,' I called back.

'No thanks,' she said. 'It's been much more fun sitting here in the pub watching you. Have you walked the whole way from Sharpham?'

'No! It was only this last bit.'

As I swam across the entrance to Bow Creek, I thought back to that day at the pub and felt an enormous temptation to turn right and swim (or even squelch) up to the pub instead. I was more than ready to end my swim, yet I hadn't even reached halfway.

After about 4k, we reached the first of two feed stations, which consisted of a floating platform in the middle of the river with marshals handing out cups of water, half bananas and jelly babies.

I clung onto the side, swallowed half a banana, and took a swig of water from a cup that was passed to me.

'I need a fresh cup!' the lady to the right of me demanded. 'These cups have already been used.'

'Yes, sorry, we are trying to reduce wastage,' said the marshal.

'I NEED AN UNUSED ONE!' she barked.

I swam away smiling to myself about the logic of someone not willing to use a cup previously used by another person, yet happy to swim for three hours in a river after heavy rain, in close proximity to 800 overly hydrated swimmers.

I put my head down and counted out another hundred strokes and then did a few minutes of breaststroke to regain my composure. Above water, the Dart was stunning. The banks of the river were thick with woodland, with lush green fields stretching over the hills above. Underwater, there was no sensation whatsoever of being on one of the most beautiful rivers in the country. These sections of breaststroke were the only enjoyable parts of my swim. I saw egrets and cormorants perched on the riverbank watching us pass; I saw kayakers and paddleboarders and people on boats; I watched children crabbing and families picnicking; I saw a heron swoop down and pluck a fish from the water (I didn't, but let's pretend I did). It was wonderful. But, tempting as it was, I didn't feel like I could do breaststroke the entire way, so plunged my head back into the murky gloom and the beauty disappeared.

I understand the logic of slower swimmers setting off first. We needed the extra time in case we ran out of water. But the major disadvantage was that all of the swimmers that started behind us were much faster. After the first ten minutes when it was only the leisurely wave swimmers in the river, the faster swimmers began to catch us up and we then spent the rest of the swim constantly being overtaken. It did little for my self-esteem.

As the first red hatted 'medium' wave swimmer passed me, I tried to up my speed, but they had disappeared out of sight before I came up for air. A few minutes later, the first of the white hatted 'fast' swimmers passed me, shortly followed by the blue 'elite' swimmers. Panic set in as, despite setting off first, I worried I was going to be the last left in the river. My heart rate quickened, and I began breathing uncontrollably, trying to swim as fast as I could to keep up with the others.

But then I had a moment of enlightenment. Firstly, there were 800 of us swimmers. I was unlikely to be the last one in the water. And secondly, and more importantly, so what if I was? Someone was going to be last, and they deserved as much praise, if not more, as whoever got out of the water first.

After I got used to the blur of different coloured hats passing me, I settled into a more comfortable rhythm. There were a few fellow yellow-hatters just in front of me, and for the previous few kilometres I seemed to be swimming at the same pace as them, which put me at ease.

On one of the long sweeping bends, I rolled onto my back to take a proper look behind me for the first time. As well as the scattering of blue, white and red hats of the faster waves who were soon to overtake me, there was also a fair number of yellow hats behind who had started at the same time as me. I was doing alright.

Occasionally, a swimmer would come past me wearing a gold swimming cap. I was fairly certain there wasn't a gold hat wave, and I had also seen a couple of gold hats amongst those in the same starting pen as me. *Perhaps they were staff, or special VIPS who paid for the privilege of a gold hat? Or maybe even celebrities?* I made a mental note to find out about these mysterious gold-hatters if I ever made it to the finish.

It takes a lot of mental discipline to be an endurance swimmer. I am not saying this in a self-congratulatory way, as I possess stubbornness, which is very different to a strong mental attitude. I found the Dart 10k perhaps as exhausting mentally as I did physically. Many, if not most, of the other swimmers seemed to be in the zone from the moment they took their first stroke until the moment they set foot on dry land. I have never reached this elusive zone while swimming.

It's a very different experience from long-distance running or cycling. There is no change in terrain or gradient; there are occasionally other obstacles such as seaweed, branches, or other swimmers, but generally every stroke is the same as the last. It must be quite a meditative feeling if you can get into that state. You catch brief glimpses of your surroundings each time you breathe, but that is only long enough to make quick calculations of direction and location, rather than any sort of sightseeing. What I am trying to politely and tactfully say is, long-distance swimming is fucking boring. Actually, it's worse than that. It is mental torture. I think you have to be very comfortable in your own head to enjoy swimming long distance, as it's a very intrapersonal activity.

Yes, it can be a lovely social activity if you swim with someone, or as part of a group. But while swimming front crawl, each time you submerge your head into the water you are trapped with just you. *Why couldn't I enjoy this time alone? Was I not able to be happy in my own company? Should solitude really be this painful?* These were all thoughts that I had while swimming down the River Dart. It was like a long and painful therapy session.

There were some occasions where I could escape this self-introspection. I lingered longer than most at the two feed stations, delighted to have my head above water and engage in small talk with other swimmers and the feed station marshals. I spoke briefly to the occasional swimmer or swim support crew as I passed, but most of the time it was a miserable and lonely experience.

This was by far the longest swim I had ever done, and therefore the longest time I had spent in my wetsuit. I had appreciated the extra buoyancy and warmth it provided for the first few miles, but now I had a general feeling of claustrophobia. The water felt like it had warmed considerably since Totnes. This was partly because I had become accustomed to the temperature, but also because the water we were swimming in was now predominately warmer seawater, rather than the cold rainwater that had been filling the river. Also, the 800 overly hydrated swimmers had no doubt dispersed some of their warm hydration. I looked enviably at the scattering of non-wetsuit swimmers who passed and wanted to rip my wetsuit off my body and be free from it.

Wetsuits are an incredible invention as they allow the

human body to stay immersed in cold water for long periods of time. But nothing compares to the feeling of cold water on your skin. And there was nothing more appealing while trapped in a wetsuit for three fucking hours.

To be a 'skin' swimmer, you have to apply for special dispensation from the OSS and prove you are an experienced cold-water skin swimmer. This suddenly felt like an important future goal, and a possible step towards my enjoyment of swimming.

It felt like I was swimming with a set of dumbbells that increased in weight every few minutes. The aching and lethargy in my arms and shoulders was horrendous, and I longed to be back on dry land. As well as feeling more and more claustrophobic because of my wetsuit, my neck was excruciating where the neoprene had rubbed against my skin. I had been warned about neck chafing, so applied a good dollop of Vaseline along the wetsuit line on my neck before the start. What I had not considered was how far the wetsuit rode up my neck while swimming. And when I did breaststroke, with my head above water, the wetsuit was all the way up at my hairline. This discomfort was an excellent incentive to keep my head down, as breaststroke was now a lot more painful than crawl.

I had told Rachel not to come along to watch. Open water swimming is not an ideal spectator sport as everyone looks the same in a wetsuit, swimming hat and goggles. And even when swimmers have emerged from the water, it is often hard to identify them. Rachel had agreed and said she was going to take the kids for a walk instead.

But two hours and 7k into the swim, I really hoped they would be there at the finish. Not for them to revel in my accomplishment, but because of the swell of emotion I was already feeling. This intensified when I rounded the final corner and caught my first glimpse of the finish in the distance. A giant floating *Dart 10k* sign sat in the water, a little way off the shore at the village of Dittisham. All along the shore, I could make out crowds of spectators lining the banks of the river.

With the end now in sight, I felt a vast sense of both delight and relief. The finish was still a way off, but for the first time I knew now that I would make it. The fear that I had tried to silence as much as possible over the previous few months was replaced with a feeling of elation. I became a little choked up with emotion and did a weird noise that was part sob, part cough, and part laugh. The swimmer to my right looked at me with concern. I raised a hand in the air and cheered, and she did the same.

Part of me wanted to race to the shore to get it over with as soon as possible, but I was too tired so continued my mixture of crawl and breaststroke as we neared the finish. I took a moment to look around and try to enjoy the moment as much as possible.

The River Dart is extremely wide here and, over to our

left, I could see the beautiful Greenway Estate perched magnificently on the riverbank. The white Georgian house was the summer home of Agatha Christie. During the second world war, American troops were stationed here while practising for the Normandy landings.

Greenway's boathouse – officially known as Sir Walter Raleigh's boathouse – sits below the house on the banks of the river. Agatha and her husband Max Mallowan were relocated to the boathouse during the war to make way for the soldiers. Don't feel sorry for her. The boathouse is bigger than most people's houses and is perhaps more appealing than the main building.

When I signed up to my Ironman, days after spinal surgery, my only actual goal was to get as far as the start line. It was just an incentive to stimulate my recovery and avoid feeling sorry for myself. I wasn't afraid of receiving a Did Not Finish. It wasn't until I made it as far as the start line that finishing became my new goal. It is often the prospect of a DNF – or more specifically, the fear of failure – that holds us back. It is that voice in our ear, whispering 'you can't do that'; that lingering self-doubt that prevents us from finding out what we are truly capable of. You'll never know unless you try.

There is no shame in a Did Not Finish, because behind every DNF is someone who started. Someone who signed up, committed, and gave it a go. And a Did Not Finish is always preferable to a Did Not Start.

It took an age to reach the shore. I could now make out the wet-suited swimmers, staggering up the red carpet to receive their hot chocolate. Oh, the hot chocolate! I had forgotten about that. The thought of that warm, sweet drink given to all finishers gave me an extra burst of energy.

When I was seemingly within standing depth of the shore, I made the same schoolboy error I had in the Plymouth Breakwater Swim of trying to put my feet down too early, which resulted in me disappearing underwater momentarily, flailing my arms erratically in the air, before resuming my swimming strokes and trying to act like nothing had happened.

Those final few strokes took every last ounce of effort, as my fingertips eventually made contact with the muddy riverbed, and I knew I was safe to stand up. A lady next to me rose to her feet and promptly collapsed back into the water. She tried again, this time maintaining her balance. My legs felt devoid of life, too. I was extremely light-headed, but I stumbled clumsily onto the shore, where I was greeted by one of the OSS marshals.

'Congratulations,' she said.

'Thank you. I've just swum 10 kilometres. I can't believe it.'

I suddenly felt a little teary. She then gave me a big hug which caught me by surprise and was a little unexpected considering I had just climbed out of a river. It was a lovely touch and made me choke up even more. I thought it was a one-off hug just for me, until I looked around and realised each of the wonderful marshals were indulging in soggy hugs with all the swimmers. To then be handed a commemorative tin mug filled with warm hot chocolate, made for an especially memorable end to what had been an incredibly tough three hours.

I then heard the familiar voices of my children and looked up to see Rachel and the kids standing amongst the spectators. It was wonderful to see them, but they were all slightly less forthcoming with the hugs.

'You did it,' said Rachel. 'I knew you would. 10k? That's amazing. I'm so impressed.'

'Thanks so much for coming,' I choked. 'I was secretly hoping you would be here.'

'Of course we were going to come. We didn't want to miss this, did we kids?'

There was no response from Layla, Leo or Kitty.

It's hard to gauge how the children feel about Rachel and me taking part in various sporting challenges. I don't think they grasp the concept of distances very well or how tough these things are. They are often quick to bring me straight back down to earth after taking part in something – such as the Dart 10k – that feels a tremendous achievement to me.

'How come it took you so long?' said Leo.

'Yeah, we've been waiting here for AGES,' said Kitty.

'Just ignore them,' said Rachel. 'They are just jealous of your hot chocolate.'

Matt and Charlie had both finished about 15 minutes ahead of me. They bumped into each other at the final feed station and then had their own little sprint to the finish. Charlie won by a couple of minutes.

'Well done, George,' said Matt. 'What did you think?'

'I hated almost every second of it. What about you?'

'I loved it. It was such fun. I will definitely do it again. Tempted?'

'Ha, no! I definitely will not be doing it again.'

'I've already got my eye on one of those gold swim hats.'

'Oh yeah, I saw those. What are they all about? How do you get one?'

'They give them to people who complete the Dart 10k three times.'

'Three times? That's crazy.'

'I'm going to sign up next year and then get my gold hat the year after that. Want to join me?'

I paused for a moment, allowing the idea to sink in.

The Dart 10k had weighed heavily on my mind for many months and been the cause of a great deal of worry and many sleepless nights. A year earlier, the prospect of swimming that far was unfathomable to me. Even at the start line that morning, it had seemed like an insurmountable challenge.

Some might see it as brave to sign up to a challenge so far outside of my comfort zone. Others might call it stupid. But it's only by testing ourselves that our comfort zone expands. Because I didn't fear the DNF – and perhaps even expected it – the boundaries of my comfort zone had been pushed further back and I discovered I was capable of far more than I realised.

But that didn't mean I wanted to do it again.

'George?' said Matt. 'I asked if you are tempted to sign up for it again next year?'

'No, sod that!' I said. 'Once is more than enough.'

Most – if not all – of the challenges and events in my books are within the reach of anyone. I am not breaking any records, attempting any 'world firsts', or taking any death-defying risks. And that's the point. I don't want you to read my books and think you could never do these things. I want you to maybe be inspired to challenge yourself, too. Push yourself that little bit further, step outside your comfort zone, and see what you can achieve.

Some of you might feel cheated or short-changed that I did finish all of the events in this book. You were perhaps expecting – or maybe even willing (thanks!) – me to fail. But just because I was done with the Dart 10k, didn't mean I had found my limit. There were many other challenges I had in mind. There will be times – perhaps many – that I take on something that I am unable to complete. And that's all part of the fun.

This is just the beginning.

I don't see this series of books as a finite project. This book will be the first of many, as I plan to take on different challenges and write about them for as long as I am able. It will be the book series that Did Not Finish. It is not about whether or not I complete these events; it is all about gaining new experiences, exploring places I've never been, feeling unfamiliar emotions, conquering fears, and hoping for plenty of adventures along the way.

And Rachel and the rest of the family will be joining me for many of them.

They just don't know that yet.

Author's note

Thank you for choosing to read my book. If you enjoyed it, I would be extremely grateful if you would consider posting a short review on Amazon and help spread the word about my books in any way you can. I realise that it is dangerous calling a book series *Did Not Finish* as it provides those who don't like it with a readymade three-word review. I'm hoping that if you are reading this bit then you did at least finish.

You can get in touch via social media:
www.facebook.com/georgemahood
www.instagram.com/georgemahood
www.twitter.com/georgemahood

Or join my mailing list on my useless website to be the first to hear about new releases.
www.georgemahood.com
Signed copies of all of my books are available in my website's 'shop'.

Did Not Finish is the first in a series of books. Please read on…

Book Two...

Did Not Try - book two in the *DNF* series - is available to order on **Amazon**.

Here is the blurb…

After signing his wife Rachel up for her first marathon without her knowledge and living to tell the tale, George is now struggling to keep up with her. He risks her wrath once again by entering her into a half-Ironman triathlon against her will: a 1.2-mile swim, 56-mile bike ride and a 13.1-mile run.

Did Not Try sees George and Rachel travel to Barcelona, Cornwall and the Cotswolds, and helps answer the age-old question: what happens when you are bursting for a wee while riding your bike, but an injured ankle means you can't unclip your cycling shoes?

Did Not Finish is a series of books about George and his family's adventures in running, cycling and swimming. From ultramarathons to triathlons, 10k swims to European cycling adventures, George promises fun and laughter every step, pedal, and paddle of the way.

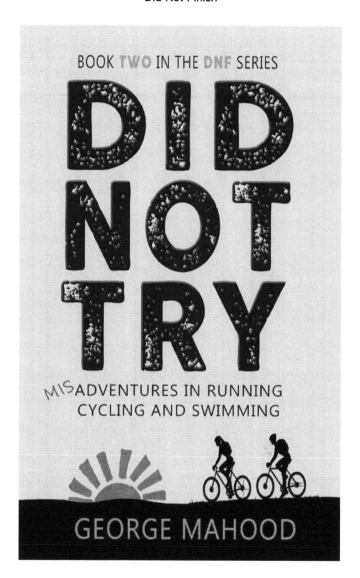

BOOK TWO IN THE DNF SERIES

DID NOT TRY

MISADVENTURES IN RUNNING
CYCLING AND SWIMMING

GEORGE MAHOOD

Acknowledgments

First thanks go to all the organisers, marshals and volunteers for putting on these races. Many of them stand outside all day in horrendous conditions, often with no reward or incentive other than the satisfaction of being a part of the event. And perhaps the joy of watching us suffer.

Special thanks to our family and friends who regularly step in to help with childcare while Rachel and I are taking part in these events.

Rachel's editing job for these books was not as scrupulous as usual, which she claimed was because she enjoyed them so much. I think that is only because she features so prominently in them. She would often write 'LOL' in the margin, even though she had been sitting next to me while reading and hadn't made a murmur. Anyway, thank you for lolling (internally).

Becky Beer was as ruthless as ever with the red pen during her proofreading. That's a compliment. Thank you! Please check out her Bookaholic Bex blog (www.bookaholicbex.wordpress.com) and Facebook page.

Thanks to Robin Hommel and Miriam for additional proofreading and feedback.

Thanks to all our friends who have taken part in these challenges and adventures with us. It is always reassuring to not be the only ones with a ridiculously stupid concept of 'fun'.

Thanks to Rachel... AGAIN (she's even got a starring role in the acknowledgements) for reluctantly agreeing to take part in many of these events with me. We are not always perfect running. cycling, swimming partners, but I wouldn't want it any other way.

Thanks to Layla, Leo and Kitty for putting up with your annoying parents and for continuing to inspire and amuse us. Hopefully one day you will look back and be glad we dragged you out on all these walks.

Thanks to my mum and dad for dragging me out on all those walks when I was younger. I didn't appreciate it at the time, but I do now.

Lastly, thanks to you for reading this series. The idea that people enjoy reading about random things I get up to still feels very bizarre to me, but I'm always honoured and grateful.

Big love.

Also by George Mahood

Free Country: A Penniless Adventure the Length of Britain

Every Day Is a Holiday

Life's a Beach

Operation Ironman: One Man's Four Month Journey from Hospital Bed to Ironman Triathlon

Not Tonight, Josephine: A Road Trip Through Small-Town America

Travels with Rachel: In Search of South America

How Not to Get Married: A no-nonsense guide to weddings… from a photographer who has seen it ALL

(available in paperback, Kindle and audiobook)

Printed in Great Britain
by Amazon